PUBLICATIONS OF RUSSELL SAGE FOUNDATION

Russell Sage Foundation was established in 1907 by Mrs. Russell Sage for the improvement of social and living conditions in the United States. In carrying out its purpose the Foundation conducts research under the direction of members of the staff or in close collaboration with other institutions, and supports programs designed to develop and demonstrate productive working relations between social scientists and other professional groups. As an integral part of its operations, the Foundation from time to time publishes books or pamphlets resulting from these activities. Publication under the imprint of the Foundation does not necessarily imply agreement by the Foundation, its Trustees, or its staff with the interpretations or conclusions of the authors.

FOUNDATIONS
20 Viewpoints

Significant papers selected from
Foundation News • Bulletin of
The Foundation Library Center

Edited, with an Introduction, by
F. EMERSON ANDREWS

Published by

RUSSELL SAGE FOUNDATION
New York *1965*

Printed in the United States
of America

Printed February, 1965
Reprinted May, 1965

Library of Congress
Catalog Card Number 65-17304

Wm. F. Fell Co., Printers
Philadelphia, Pa.

Contents

Introduction

F. EMERSON ANDREWS*

THE FOUNDATION may be described as an instrument for the contribution of private wealth to public purpose. Under this broad definition foundations, chiefly in the form of fixed charitable trusts, are older than recorded history. However, about the beginning of the twentieth century the foundation idea began to take deep root in American soil, but with a significant difference from the old concept. Large endowments were set up, often in perpetuity, but with wide latitude in their use. "To promote the well-being of mankind throughout the world," the purpose-clause of The Rockefeller Foundation, was not unusual.

Characteristically the larger American foundations have great freedom of action. Their new doctrine asserts that the funds of foundations are in part venture capital; their usual purpose is not relief or even cure, it is prevention, research, and discovery.

In the 1940's a new wave of foundations began to sweep over the country, encouraged by high levels of taxation resulting from World War II. Most of these younger organizations were family or company-sponsored foundations, both differing in one significant respect from the traditional type: usually they had no large initial corpus, but carried on their often substantial programs with moneys currently received.

Presently there are in the United States some 15,000 foundations, with assets approximating $14.5 billion, making grants in the neighborhood of $800 million annually. In so large a group of any type, abusers of privilege are certain to appear, and should be ferreted out. More important than emphasis on individual cases of abuse, however, is a balanced assessment of the place of foundations in American society.

Because foundations are numerous and some of them bear the names of wealthy families, a popular misconception exists that they have tremendous assets and are able to make almost unlimited expenditures. Relatively, the resources of foundations are not large in the American economy, and may be shrinking. In 1913 the federal government's total expenditures for education amounted to $5 million. Carnegie Corporation of New York in that

* President, The Foundation Library Center.

year spent $5.6 million, so that if it had devoted all its funds to education, it could have more than equaled the federal government total. The Rockefeller Foundation is known around the world for its extensive fellowship program, on which it has spent in the past fifty years $61 million. This is less than the American government spends today on its fellowship program in a single year, and for the fiscal year ending in 1965 the federal government's total expenditures for education are estimated at $1,691 million.

The question may fairly be asked whether the foundations' annual $800 million in grants for all purposes serves a significant function even in private philanthropy, where some $10 billion is given, chiefly by individuals.

Foundations are in some respects unique among American social institutions. They are the only important agencies in America free from the political controls of legislative appropriations and pressure groups, and free from the necessity of tempering programs to the judgments and the prejudices of current contributors. Because of this position of unusual freedom, they have an opportunity, and perhaps a special responsibility, to attack the longer-range, more difficult, and often controversial questions which face the nation and the world. They have sometimes been called the "venture capital" of philanthropy, and many of them do spend a substantial part of their funds in pioneering ventures that would have difficulty in finding support from other private sources, or from government.

For the immediate future, barring major catastrophies of war, severe inflation, or government controls, foundations may be expected to increase in number, though probably not in their relative dollar share of the American economy. But size is not of primary importance. It is important that there is, and that there shall remain in America, a type of philanthropic entrepreneur free from governmental or mass public pressures. The philanthropic foundation is such an instrument.

This small book has been issued to make readily available some of the significant and timely discussions of foundations that have appeared during the past four years in *Foundation News*, the bimonthly Bulletin issued by The Foundation Library Center. The articles, sometimes descriptive and sometimes expressions of vigorous opinion, are in all cases the views of experienced persons, often the leading authority in the field concerned.

They fall into three general categories. First are broad discussions of that extraordinary expression of American free enterprise, private philanthropy, and its ingenious invention, the freely operating philanthropic foundation. The brief report of a European conference points up certain contrasts.

Secondly, the fields in which foundations make grants are identified for three recent years, and operations in a few quite specific areas are discussed on the basis of practical experience.

Finally, a section on running foundations will be of special interest to foundation personnel and seekers of grants. This section covers a wide gamut, ranging from training foundation executives, through the intricacies of tax and legal problems, to sage advice on how to frame a persuasive grant proposal.

The editor expresses thanks to the distinguished authors for their permission to use their contributions in this form, and special appreciation to the two editors of *Foundation News*—Burton Raffel, editor for the first three years, and J. Richard Taft, editor since November, 1963—for their skill in assembling so great a wealth of fine articles that selection has been difficult. Gratitude goes to Dr. Orville G. Brim, Jr., president of Russell Sage Foundation, for originating this project and to the Foundation for undertaking it.

It may be appropriate to repeat for this collection the wish expressed for *Foundation News* in its Beginning Note: "It is hoped that this [publication] may serve both those who disburse and those who seek foundation funds, and promote a better understanding of this unique instrument for the contribution of private wealth to public purpose."

Part I

THE GENERAL SCENE

Philanthropy as a Social Investment

EVERETT CASE*

AMONG THE BASIC FREEDOMS which we claim as American citizens, the freedom to give is seldom, if ever, mentioned. Nevertheless, it is a freedom which, as citizens, we will doubtless be exercising this year to the tune of some $10 billions. Its exercise is subject, moreover, to none of the artificial limitations which still hedge, in varying degree, the general enjoyment of certain other civil rights. And the figure I cite refers to private philanthropy only. Whether or not this is sharply distinguished from government largesse, either at home or abroad, it is small wonder that American philanthropy has come to be regarded as one of the distinctive and, indeed, creative contributions of our culture.

Ten billion dollars, to be sure, is hardly more than 2 per cent of the total personal income of the American people, and it is only about 10 per cent of our current federal budget. Its strategic importance, however, is not to be measured in arithmetic terms, for the elimination of our private philanthropy would leave an economic, social, and moral vacuum of very large dimensions.

True, government revenues would doubtless rise somewhat if the tax benefits attached to certain kinds of gifts were also eliminated, but if government set out to fill the vacuum itself, the rise in costs would be disproportionately sharp. Besides, there are constitutional barriers to government support of churches, for example, which now rank first among the several beneficiaries of voluntary giving. With respect to schools, colleges, and hospitals, moreover, you would likewise resist as a citizen any abrogation of your freedom to direct your gift dollars, for example, to "the college of your choice." Indeed, this freedom which we take so much for granted turns out, upon examination, to be pretty close to basic, and it would be a curious sort of free society that attempted to deny it.

Fortunately, the encouragement of private philanthropy is today an integral part of public policy as reflected in our tax laws, federal and state. Evidently an overwhelming majority of our legislative representatives

* President, Alfred P. Sloan Foundation. Mr. Case's remarks are adapted from an address before the Greater Cleveland Associated Foundation, 29 October 1963.

firmly believe that, in our philanthropic as well as in our business and political concerns, there is virtue in the diffusion rather than the concentration of the decision-making power. This is in notable and obvious contrast to the organization of Soviet society, where the social surplus, if any, is allocated by governmental fiat. I suggest it is one of many contrasts in which we, as Americans, can take pride. If this particular contrast ever becomes less vivid, let it be because of a change in Soviet rather than American policy, even though the latter appears in the guise of tax "reform." . . .

Problems of Growth

Looking at the foundations, one realizes that their proliferation has been a phenomenon of recent times; according to The Foundation Library Center, they now number somewhat more than 15,000, with estimated total assets of some $14 billions. To be sure, the growth in their resources over the years has hardly exceeded the expansion of total philanthropic giving, or perhaps of the economy itself. Nevertheless, in view of the many new foundations, great and small, that have appeared since the close of World War II, it should hardly surprise us to find that here and there abuses may have crept in, of the kind that usually attaches to the exponential growth of any human enterprise. The *Wall Street Journal*, indeed, has suggested that certain leaders of our churches are disturbed lest excessive zeal for high returns may have involved some of our church organizations and religious foundations unduly in commercial activities.

Obviously it is to the interest of every responsible foundation, and of every citizen, that these abuses be identified and eliminated; and if our congressional investigators, including Mr. Patman, will do precisely that, they will have rendered an important public service. In such a task, however, the responsible reformer will always be mindful of two fundamentals: first, the need to distinguish between the stubborn reality and the mere allegation of abuse; second, the need to present the total picture in its true colors and perspective. If either of these canons be flouted, the effect can be only to mislead and inflame a public which can be expected to render a fair judgment only as it is fully and honestly informed. And here, I submit, the foundations have certain responsibilities of their own.

A Reasonable Perspective

What then would we regard as a fair perspective so far as foundations are concerned? First, let us remember that in the whole spectrum of private philanthropy, foundation grants now account for only some 8 per cent of the annual total, more than 85 per cent of which comes from individual gifts and bequests, with the other 6 or 7 per cent now coming from the corporations. If, then, we were to eliminate the endowed foundations altogether, private philanthropy would lose, on the face of it, only $1 out of every $12 at its disposal. But before concluding that this loss would be inconsequential, we would do well to analyze a bit more carefully the dynamic relationship of this particular segment to the whole.

Now, the very creation of a foundation (other than corporate) reflects the decision of some individual or family to transmute a private fortune into a public trust, typically for the benefit of future as well as present generations. Granted that the decision may be prompted by diverse motives and considerations, the end result is essentially the same: a kind of institutional extension of the individual's freedom to give. The basic difference is that, by means of the foundation, this freedom—and the obligations which it entails—is shared or turned over completely to a board of trustees which, under the terms of its charter, assumes full legal and moral responsibility for the care and nourishment of its assets and the disbursement of its income—and, it may be, of its capital as well—always for the benefit of the public.

On the creation of such a social instrument for the encouragement, perpetuation, and disinterested direction of private philanthropy, a free and enlightened society has good and obvious reasons to congratulate itself. By the same token, it will do well to establish such safeguards against its abuse as will conserve the social effectiveness of the instrument itself, taking every care not to limit needlessly the freedom of the honest administrator because of the sins of the irresponsible few. Certainly society should stipulate, as it does, the terms and conditions for establishing such public trusts and should expect—and if necessary, demand—a periodic and public accounting of their administration.

But if foundations have their very roots in the individual's freedom to give, the strategic nature of their grants may enormously enhance their potentialities for good. They have the opportunity and the obligation not merely to be selective about the appeals to which they respond, but also to take the initiative in searching out those special situations in which their grants are likely to be most productive of significant benefits to society as a whole.

The Sound Investment

This, of course, is the nub of the matter. It is at once the most important and difficult problem confronting foundations. I say this because, in the nature of things, the well organized foundation has an almost unique opportunity to perform for non-profit enterprise a function analogous to that which the venture capitalist performs for our economy.

Always the astute venture capitalist is busily scanning the horizon for the kind of opportunity in which the successful exploitation of a new product, with the promise of very high returns, waits chiefly upon the provision of risk capital in adequate amounts. He makes his investment, however, only when he is satisfied that *capital is the one missing ingredient* in a complex that includes sound management (which occasionally he may wish to install), a promising idea or product, and the necessary manufacturing and marketing skills. . . .

Now the wisest venture capitalist makes mistakes and so, heaven knows, do the foundations. Even our most conspicuous successes, moreover, may themselves create new and stubborn problems. Foundation-supported medical programs, which have greatly reduced infant mortality and prolonged life expectancy, have undoubtedly contributed to the population pressures from which certain Asiatic countries now suffer more acutely than ever. Nevertheless, the vast progress made since the turn of the century toward the conquest of malaria, hookworm, and illiteracy, owes much to the pioneering efforts of The Rockefeller Foundation and Carnegie Corporation of New York; and the vastly increased productivity of Mexican agriculture, deriving from another Rockefeller venture, affords fresh hope to the many other nations that currently suffer from an inadequate food supply.

My own experience compels me to add that it is hard to overstate all that our college and university faculties—and so the cause of higher education—owe to Ford's massive salary grants of the mid-fifties. Intrinsically helpful as they were, they were also so successful in dramatizing a critical need as to release the flow of the other funds required to meet it. Is a built-in multiplier the secret weapon of the bold and timely grant?

But the needs of human beings are unlimited, and since the resources of no foundation—not even Ford—can be stretched very far toward meeting them, the search for areas of key concern that promise the highest return on current investment is at once restless and never ending.

Thus, the trustees of both the Ford and Rockefeller foundations have recently completed major policy reviews, resulting in a fresh definition of each foundation's primary fields of concern. It is important for others, including the Sloan Foundation, to be aware of such developments, lest all of us bow to current fashions and put all of our philanthropic eggs in one basket. . . .

Foundations and the Government:
Some Observations on the Future

MORTIMER M. CAPLIN*

AT ONE TIME, I considered myself something of an expert on foundations. As an attorney, I have helped to organize them. I have served as a foundation consultant, and as a foundation trustee. My sympathies, then, if not any great fund of knowledge, are attuned to your problems. And my present position as Commissioner of Internal Revenue is a distinctly dual one, since the Commissioner not only administers a far-flung agency having some 60,000 employees but, just as importantly, he operates as the only non-civil servant in that agency. In this sense he represents taxpayer interests as well as those of the government—and this aspect of my job is one I personally take most seriously. I want to make sure that we are taking account of what is convenient for the taxpayer, and are refraining from overzealousness. I am striving to develop a real measure of reasonableness in our operations—in short, to stand for good sense and balance as well as for the long arm of the collector of taxes.

Congress, and the People

Congressman Patman's recent inquiries have once again turned the spotlight onto foundations and their place in our society. I need not rehearse his findings, both tentative and definite, except to indicate that, in his view, the Internal Revenue Service is not the proper agency to exercise truly effective supervisory control. This also happens to be my own view, if the kind of supervision and control exercised, for example, by the Securities and Exchange Commission over investment companies and public utility holding companies, should ever become necessary.

Public attention has, however, been directed toward foundations, with a strongly issued invitation that a long, close look be taken. How does the Revenue Service fit into this developing picture? I think it fair to say that

* Partner in the law firm Caplin, Battle & Harris, Washington, D.C.; Chairman of Executive Committee, Prentice-Hall, Inc.; formerly Commissioner of Internal Revenue. These remarks are based upon an address before The Foundations Luncheon Group, New York City, delivered 31 January 1963.

before 1961, certainly, our audit pattern was rather heavily oriented toward the "most productive" situations—i.e., toward an examination of those tax returns where deficiencies seemed most likely. This was a rather short-sighted approach. Of the more than $99 billion collected in taxes last year, fully 97 per cent was either voluntary or pre-collected as withholding. No country in the world can match such a record of compliance—it is truly the heart of our taxing system. Taking the longer view, I concluded, shortly after becoming Commissioner, that what was most needed, and what the Revenue Service could most usefully help to accomplish, was a further strengthening of public confidence in our taxing system. By looking into areas of abuse, and of potential abuse, we seek to build public confidence in the overall fairness of American taxation and establish in the public mind a sense of administration without favoritism, across the board.

The Internal Revenue Service

Accordingly, the Revenue Service has modified its audit pattern. We are examining much more heavily in areas which may indeed produce no deficiencies, and thus no revenue for the government, because we feel that the public at large needs assurance that everyone is being checked into—and on some reasonable cyclical basis. I am, of course, referring to more than foundations alone: all tax-exempt organizations are covered in the expanded audit program.

What have we found, inquiring into foundation practices? There have been abuses. We have found self-dealing between the foundation and insider groups; some losses of exemption have resulted. We have found unreasonable accumulations. We have found speculative investments—such things as third mortgages on Florida real estate and the so-called "ABC" oil transactions. We have found foundations actually going out and competing for interest income, and for rental income. We have even found manipulation of leases, with the obvious purpose of evading the "business lease" provisions of the tax laws, applicable to certain leases of at least five years in duration. In short, we have found a wide variety of transactions close to, as well as on the other side of, legality—violations of the spirit, if not always of the letter, of the law. Congressman Patman's investigations have been of considerable assistance—and impetus—to us, in these matters.

New Directions

Our program for more effective supervision in the foundation field has three main prongs. First, the annual information return filed with the Revenue Service, Form 990-A, has been revised. Reporting requirements for 1962 and subsequent years have been expanded, and virtually all of the information to be submitted will henceforth be open to public inspection. I think this expanded disclosure alone will have a very healthy impact in areas of abuse.

Second, there is the expanded audit program I mentioned previously. Whereas in past years there have been perhaps 2,000 audits per year in the tax-exempt organization field, there will now be 10,000 per year. This means that all foundations should be prepared for an audit, perhaps this year, perhaps next. We seek your help in making the audit as fair and as expeditious as possible. Inevitably, our staff is less familiar than it should be with foundations; our expertise is far greater in other areas. We are attempting to correct this by developing training programs and instructional materials for our people. When we are in contact with you—and we will be—please be as careful, and as helpful, and as patient, as you can.

Third, and as yet least definite, is the matter of legislative study and proposals. A White House inter-agency task force has already done some preliminary investigation of the whole area and its findings have been referred to the Treasury Department, following preliminary analysis. The Treasury will shortly announce a broadly-based advisory group, to consult with and advise it on possible legislative action. Government people and non-government people will be represented. The Revenue Service is conducting certain studies, and we will refer our findings to the advisory group. Specific proposals can be expected later on.

Self-policing

I have every hope that harsh corrective legislation will not be necessary. One wholesome substitute would be an effective program of self-policing by foundations. Other tax-exempt groups have already begun such programs. The college fund-raisers, for example, have been much concerned about certain abuses occurring within their ranks. After holding meetings on the subject, they are pressing for effective measures of self-policing. Studies are under way—in which, let me point out, the Revenue Service is cooperating—and experienced consultants are to be hired. Art museums and art association directors have also been disturbed by abuses arising from over-valuation of donated art objects, and will take steps to correct them. So too, will dealers in rare manuscripts. And so on.

Legislation now on the books provides a good deal of room for more vigorous enforcement on our part. We intend to be vigorous; we have the responsibility to be. But the foundations can, as I say, do a great deal to help both us and themselves. I would suggest five courses of action:

(1) Foundations should strive to foster public trust in their operations. I am not thinking so much of mere publicity as I am of disclosure and of an awareness that public trust is something to be avidly sought. Foundations should both act and speak in a manner which recognizes that they have been charged with a public trust and are obligated to live up to it.

(2) Foundations should not simply obey the law—or, rather, they should not confine themselves to avoiding its penalties. Borderline transactions, strictly legal perhaps, but in spirit running distinctly against the statutory grain, should be as carefully shunned as are clearly proscribed transactions. In other words, foundations should strive to understand and cooperate with the law, rather than to outwit or to take advantage of it.

(3) Foundations should file information returns with the federal (and where required the state) government which are in all respects unexceptionable—clear, complete, accurate, and timely. Few things are more basic to public trust than public knowledge.

(4) When the Revenue Service initiates audit procedures, foundations should cooperate to the fullest extent possible. The Service should not be thought of as alien or inimical to foundation operations. Both sides have their jobs to do; both sides should endeavor to fulfill all obligations in an atmosphere of mutual respect and understanding.

(5) Foundations should give serious thought to the formulation of a specific code of conduct. I am not proposing a trade association, or the merging of individual identities into some sort of semi-collective entity. But the precise standards which foundations should observe, in commonly experienced situations, have yet to be articulated. It seems to me desirable that the foundations themselves make—and then observe—such a formulation. I believe that such a recognized code would be a giant step forward in establishing the kind of meaningful program of self-policing I am advocating.

The promotion of private philanthropy through tax forgiveness is a basic tenet of the United States tax system. That basic tenet is not threatened by the President's current tax proposals, nor is it endangered by the Revenue Service's current enforcement program. What could cause serious and untoward developments, it seems to me, would be the failure of the foundations themselves to live up to their role—the role envisaged for them by the spirit of our tax laws and increasingly insisted upon by the American public.

The Economic Function of Foundations

PHILIP S. BROUGHTON*

NO INSTITUTIONS have ever developed into mature effectiveness without suffering a good many slings and arrows. If foundations have been uncomfortable since the successive inquiries of Cox and Reece and Patman, and the IRS, they now have a better understanding of how others may see them, —others, that is, who are not wholly entranced.

The foundation officer in the beginning was a benign doer of good. He was the giver of scholarships in a society which did not regard universal unlimited education either as a natural right or an economic and military necessity. He was fighting external enemies—the boll weevil, pellagra, malaria, infant mortality—accepted as the common enemies of all. To *do good* was to give alms and to sequester the poor and the orphan, not to examine the causes and cure of poverty or broken homes.

As philanthropic practice turned from palliatives to inquiry into underlying causes, the new focus carried an implicit criticism of society and its arrangements. It is small wonder that foundations came under attack. There is no obsolescent structure—social, economic, institutional, or politic—but someone has a vested interest in it. The makers of buggy whips were not in the vanguard of the fight for better automobile roads. The voters, heavily overrepresented in a rural gerrymander, take unkindly to a scholarly study of legislative apportionment. Criticism came from many sources. And, as is usual in democratic society, a series of analytical commentaries in defense of foundations have come from officers and trustees. A new mood of self-examination is with us. Let us identify three main lines of criticism.

The first has to do with integrity and propriety. With more than 15,000 foundations of record, there must be some so ill-staffed, so small in resources, so responsive to personal whim, so contrived for mere tax avoidance, so without demonstrated public service program, that they are deplorable. There would be some sour apples in any business with 15,000 units. Certainly, it would be helpful to the reputation of all legitimate foundations if legal quackeries masquerading as foundations were eliminated.

* Secretary, The A. W. Mellon Educational and Charitable Trust.

The second group of criticisms has to do with policy and management procedure, the nature and quality of foundation programs. Do foundations give too much to health, too much to education, too much to research? Do they give too little for endowment, buildings, general operations, or too much? Are they timorous? Are they too obsessed with the experimental? Are they bureaucratic? These are policy and management issues of the kind that plague every business and every public institution. Constant scrutiny of operations is the price of productivity in any field.

The third is an attack upon the economic function of foundations in our economy: a denial or implied denial that they contribute to the dynamics of the management of public service institutions, institutions which have a singular tendency to become lethargic, bureaucratic, non-innovative. In this third area of attack, the fork has a public and a private prong.

Prong One: Let government do it all. As put by one of Leo Szilard's dolphins, he "was puzzled why money which would otherwise be taxed away . . . should be permitted to go to foundations when obviously foundations never did anything worthwhile except what the government was doing anyway and, in many cases, was doing better."[1]

Prong Two: Give money, or most of it, to the general funds of established institutions. Foundations (this argument runs) divert money from the basic endowments of hospitals, universities, museums, opera, and welfare agencies. Foundations apply this money to new and experimental activities, thus depriving the responsible trustees of financing for on-going activities.

It is to this third criticism—the challenge to economic function—that this paper is addressed. Both attacks—one from the governmental sector, one from the private sector—question the economic usefulness of the foundation as an instrument of our economy. Let us examine it.

Choice is Freedom

There is a logic of freedom which at its simplest level is as inescapable as geometry, or perhaps in these days of higher mathematics, one should say, as inexorable as geometry once seemed. Freedom is the ability to choose, to have a choice. All the growth and innovation and originality, all the creativity in the affairs of men reflect this: the freedom to choose.

One wonders why this simple fact is not more frequently employed to destroy the pretensions of communism. Certain earnest patriots work so hard to attack doctrines, to expose ideological outrages, to denounce in apoplectic terms the language of Khrushchev or Stalin or Lenin that they become doctrinaire themselves. "Whom the Gods would destroy, they first

[1] *The Voice of the Dolphins,* Simon and Schuster, New York, 1961, p. 43.

make mad." We would do much better to boil the issue down to the problem of the individual man: the creative man with a new idea and what he can do with it.

What he can do with his idea in a free society is traditionally clear. If it is simple, he can develop it himself. If it requires investment beyond his means, he can borrow, or he can sell stock, or he can take partners on an agreed relationship. If it is too big for such individual action, he can license, or sell, or contract the development of his idea with any one of several producers. Our technique is not perfect in every respect, but the intent of our laws—our anti-trust laws, our tax laws, our laws of incorporation—is to keep the channels of choice open to assure freedom of the innovator, the man with the idea, to give him a choice of roads.

By contrast, the Soviet economy, or any communist or totalitarian economy, is completely "rationalized." There is a single channel. Step by step one must move up through the established lines of the appropriate commissariat. If someone says, "No," "Nyet," or assigns the idea to a bureaucratic pigeonhole, the innovator may at his own risk write an indignant letter to Pravda. But he can't get five friends to invest their capital and go into competition with The Establishment. His idea, his innovation is dead. That's that. There is no choice, no alternative. The Russians have discovered this does not work well, and since the November, 1962 meeting of the Communist party, a new Soviet economic literature on productivity and innovation has developed.

Within our social policy of *choice*, of *decision*, of *selection*, to use Adler's three synonyms, there is a special element which helps to assure freedom.[1] That element is diversity: the encouragement and stimulation of many units with a variety of individual policy, program, and emphasis. All our laws protecting small business are based on this social policy. The competition of units and of diverse forms of organization, sources of financing, of supply, and of marketing channels is a basic principle of the free economy.

So far I have been talking economics, economics so elementary that my only defense is Justice Holmes' dictum that, more than new discovery, we need education in the obvious. For it is in the obvious economics that the literature of the foundation field is lacking. We find books and essays on philanthropy, modern and ancient, religious and secular. The motives of

[1] "The word 'choice' or a synonym of it, such as 'decision' or 'selection' is used by typical proponents of natural freedom. . . . A man is free, they claim, only when the circumstances under which he acts are such that he could have acted otherwise had he wished to. According to their view, an environment favorable to freedom is one which provides and permits alternative courses of action." Adler, Mortimer, *The Idea of Freedom*, Doubleday and Co., New York, 1958, vol. 1, p. 401.

giving have been analyzed; the accounting, the investments, the legal responsibilities, the tax problems; but nowhere do we seem to find any comprehensive discussion of the economic function of foundations in preserving a free society marked by choice, decision, selection. "Seed money," "risk capital of philanthropy," "social investment" are all old foundation phrases, but, as too often used, they seem defensive justification of special intervention instead of describing an essential part of a normal economic process. What we need is some grubby economics about the relation of foundation practice to good public management. An examination of economic function might deeply affect both foundation policy and its public acceptance.

The Need for Diversity

To begin with, let us admit that the man with the idea, the innovator, is seldom the individual investigator exemplified by the early Henry Ford, the early Edison, the Wright Brothers, Goodyear and his pan of accidentally vulcanized rubber. As Chester Barnard has spelled it out for us, the condition of man is organization. Creative man, whether he be inventor or creative manager, is part of a complex institution. His relation to organization is the problem. Opportunity, enabling the creative man to function, must be provided for in an organizational context.

The more complex society becomes, the more the growth and execution of ideas depends on organized relationships. Technology and education are costly. Competing demands for money within an organization always assure us that keeping within normal budgeted income will be difficult. The distribution of money from any single source becomes patterned. Increasingly, the freedom of selective decision depends on a diversity of sources of finance. Without that diversity there is no choice. For brevity, let us use the colleges as illustration of this point. The problem of innovation and choice is analogous for hospitals, for social agencies, for the arts, or any other institution.

1. It is a common observation that no institution can be wholly free if it is totally dependent on government support. This is especially true in our country, for however seldom legislatures overtly interfere with academic freedom, no university administration is unaware of legislative attitude. More important, legislatures are usually tone deaf to the innovative changes creative leadership would recommend.

Legislatures in their design of grant-making procedures, do not deal with policy, but with trivia. Today's tendency in Congress, for example, is to demand meticulous accounting; even a research grant becomes a contract demanding defined demonstrable results on a set schedule. With dependence on federal or state funds, under present policies the research which led to the Salk and Sabin vaccines would not have been possible. Moreover, federal funds reflect a program preoccupation which could in time distort the idea of a university. He who pays the piper, calls the tune.

2. A few institutions throughout the country are predominantly supported by a single donor or group of donors. They are free to whatever extent the vision and resources of the donor may go. The range is broad, from the dedicated group with convictions about education who contribute to St. John's, to one donor who stated privately that for "his college" he reads and approves every textbook in the social sciences. At another extreme a few colleges base their donor appeal on religious or economic conformity to donor opinion, hardly an enduring basis for creativity.

3. There is no more challenging task than building a loyal constituency for a college, whether among few or many private donors. But the organized alumni and other broad community campaigns are at best a collateral support, hardly dependable for creative innovative capital. Such contributors may respond to creative leadership; they may also be repelled by needed change.

4. As for tuition: tuition never meets the need any more than memberships support an art museum.

5. And whoever heard of an endowment that was big enough to support innovation? Even Harvard, with an endowment of nearly $900,000,000 (market), wouldn't innovate to the extent of establishing a new professorship in so pressing a field as population studies, without new fund raising for the particular chair. It is a nice policy if you can manage it.

Mounting costs of operation, mounting pressures of numbers, the educational needs of our complex society, and our confused inability to set selective quality standards for those who enter college, are all factors that make it difficult to meet the budget, let alone provide innovative funds.

Someone you meet may need to have this spelled out. You are a dean or a college president with only these sources, and there comes to you a professor or a group of your faculty with an important idea. It may be a piece of research. It may be a new approach to teaching or the curriculum, or the urgent need for building a library collection in a crucial field. Whatever it is, it is expensive. As you listen, you are convinced it is truly significant. Then you remember that the very able head of the Greek department is getting only $8,500 a year and has five children, that the library has had to let its subscription to a score of scholarly periodicals lapse for sheer lack of funds, and over in the chemistry department the program is going to pieces for inadequate and out-of-date equipment.

Now, ask yourself as a creative administrator, do you have freedom, do you have choice? Can you make a selection or a decision based upon priorities of creative innovation? No. You are the prisoner of the urgencies.

If these were all your sources, creativity would have a hard time of it. The urgencies, the necessities, the budget of normal income preclude many five or six digit allocations of funds to the innovator. Moreover, we live in a society where the cost of innovation may run to seven or eight digits. (That may be easier to raise because it is dramatic.)

I suggest that in the public sector (by which I mean both the governmental and the tax-exempt public service institutions) there is at present only one way that enough money can be found for creative change: that is to have diversified pools of funds, out of reach of the routine urgencies, available primarily for innovation. That is the historic and primary role of foundations in the economy. So administered, they do not interfere with institutional policy. They free management for choices of policy which would otherwise be unavailable.

The Enabling Concept of Grants

I have, as you see, small sympathy for those who condemn foundations, willy nilly, on the ground that they look for the new, the creative, the demonstration, the pilot program. Redirect major funds into programs of ordinary support for needy institutions, and you would take a long step toward limiting the choice, the selection, the decision, the freedom of creative institutional leadership. But note, too, the wise foundation does not free-lance. These are funds *to enable* creative management to act. Let us look at some examples:

1. Begin with a hypothetical case. You have in your university a medical center which is ill-supported financially, dominated by an "old guard" most of whom graduated thirty years before, and are against any change, especially change which does not at the same time confirm their dominance. There are no full-time clinical professors, the loosely "associated medical center hospitals" are dominated by a part-time faculty which enjoys the prestige and prosperity of a closed corporation.

Under such a pattern you have no freedom of choice. Regular funds and general contributions would be available not for pioneering but for the *status quo*. As a university president you would not be blind to the fact that the opposition includes most of the beloved family physicians of your own trustees.

How often has university leadership met this kind of "old order"? How often has that old order been outflanked by the fact that available independent funds had financed innovative post-graduate education, teaching, or hospital service programs which by their very character made the old order untenable? Hypothetical, did I say? I know of three such cases. They occurred within 500 miles of where I live and all within the last fifteen years.

2. Or take a concrete case, the leadership of Dr. Calvin Gross as Pittsburgh Superintendent of Public Schools. Like most metropolitan school systems, its urgencies were great; its needs were closely budgeted. The bureaucratic rigidities, the seniority power patterns of a school system are not conducive to innovation, even to minor innovation.

When a creative administrator such as Dr. Gross comes into an old system, he finds all the limitations of money and policy and organization in patterns peculiar to the system. Most administrators butt their heads against the brick wall for a time, dislodge a few bricks, and then either move on or succumb to the routine. Foundation grants, many of them quite small, helped when Dr. Gross identified specific areas of breakthrough and requested assistance. Grants were enabling. They freed Dr. Gross to give him *choice, selection, decision.* Dr. Gross' need would have had little prospect of financing from normal appropriating bodies. Only because there were sources of independent funds was he free to move.

One of the great satisfactions in such giving in the governmental sector is that a small grant makes a large impact. Over the years millions of dollars of taxpayers' money will be better spent, tens of thousands of children will be better educated.

3. Consider also the changes that have occurred in the quality of the University of Pittsburgh. Chancellor Litchfield has won admiration for the way he has successfully tackled tough problems of long standing. But rest assured that if all the money that Pitt received had simply been part of an unearmarked endowment prior to the time Dr. Litchfield took office, he would not have had so great freedom to organize new choices, decisions, selections.

This concept of foundation grants as enabling has one stern requirement: I know no way in which a grant can produce results in institutions or communities when the leadership does not come from within. The problem parallels the story of the three boy scouts who helped the old lady across the street. It took three because she didn't want to go. There are such boy scouts among foundations.

Capital Formation; A Key Distinction

These illustrations of economic function point to a basic difference between the financing of the public sector and the private sector of our economy. That difference is the availability of innovative capital in the two sectors. Success in business means income for growth and a base for capital expansion. A successful program in government or a public service institution means merely greater expenditures; and even the largest beneficiaries resent the taxes.

In the private sector the mechanisms of capital formation are built in. Creative innovation is an imperative. One must have the capital, the will and the freedom to use it—or lose the competitive struggle to someone with the courage and imagination and capital to innovate.

Private management knows this and therefore does not distribute all its income as dividends nor divide it to the last cent between dividends and labor; income is plowed back into the business for growth, i.e. innovation. Under defined circumstances new securities may be issued, money invested or borrowed, assets mortgaged. The means to form capital and the pressure to use it for innovation are the dynamics of the private sector.

In the public sector of the economy the cards are stacked against creative management as the instrument of change. There are no built-in mechanisms of capital formation. Any growth increments which derive from good government, for example, become the assets of the private economy (just as bad government becomes the burden of that economy). Moreover, financial controls in the public sector are instruments of scrutiny, routine, and precedent, the arch enemies of creative innovation, productivity, and change. Administrative management or legislatures, the processes primarily reflect distrust.

Consider the contributions of public administration: the process of budget review, of audit. They were designed to reassure the taxpayer (or the Community Chest donor) that the public service institution was pinching every penny. The symbols of productivity give way to the symbols of scrutiny. It is innovation, not routine precedent, that is constantly challenged.

Or, turn to the process of review by legislatures and by institutional or Community Chest boards, processes well designed to assure the defeat of innovation. Members have deep roots in the *status quo* which put them where they are. In our public life and in the politics of our institutions it is easy to mobilize opposition to change: the staff who have job tenure, the beneficiaries, the communities with a useless army installation, the wraith of a dead statesman or the wrath of a founding donor. No innovative capital for creative management, only proven routines. If one closes the buggy whip inspection service, he destroys jobs.

There is, of course, in both the governmental and the public service sector another kind of change: change responsive to emotional causes.

Millions for a political panacea. Millions for a dramatic disease. Military competition changes all the rules: the Dolphin's sarcasm about foundations reflects Dr. Szilard's experience. His fame and his grants related to our competition with the Soviet. Be first to split the atom, and you too will have unbounded faith in government as the source of research funds. But such processes have nothing to do with innovative capital enabling management to improve the productivity of an institution, the job that in the private sector management must do or perish.

And if you want to test this analysis, consider two cases: one in the private and one in the public sector. First, the railroads: in the first half of this century they had imposed upon them through regulation the scrutinizing, retrenching, routinizing financial patterns which normally characterize government. For fifty years ingenuity went into justifying and defending rate bases and costs, instead of lowering them through innovation. Only competition from the highways and the air brought new innovative thinking. Second, public education which has lately found new opportunity for excellence. Innovation is sought and welcomed largely because Sputnik applied to our educational system the competitive pressures to produce which private business faces every year.

Public or private, the dynamics of productivity is wise innovation, change through enabling creative management to do its job. Such innovation requires capital which is not usually available to public sector institutions through their normal sources of funds. Foundations have as a central responsibility making such enabling funds available; they are, in effect, the investment bankers of the public sector. Without foundation sources public sector institutions would become more routine, more bureaucratic, and more unproductive.

As a cold economic statement, this may seem to be a non-charitable description of foundation philanthropy. But, without such economic function, few charitable institutions would be as productive as they are. In the hands of government, in the vaults of general endowments, these funds would not perform this economic function.

European Foundations*

THE ROYAUMONT working group on European foundations, with representatives from 8 European countries (Belgium, Denmark, Finland, France, Germany, Holland, Luxembourg, and the United Kingdom) and 5 international agencies, was confronted with fairly clear evidence that the fiscal and other legal privileges accorded foundations and philanthropy vary enormously from country to country. In France, for example, substantially no concessions to charity are made; special laws even provide for reexamination of inter vivos gifts, when estates are being settled. England's chief subsidy is the complex and cumbersome seven-year covenant device: British courts have never been anxious to extend the meaning of "charity," so that many purposes popularly regarded as charitable are not charitable in English law. In Belgium, where foundations must be created via a central government statute, charitable deductions are not allowed to industry for contributions of any sort, unless given to certain named universities; the same is true for individuals. Since South African companies are chiefly foreign owned, tax exemptions are liberal, but heavy "contributions" are expected for those charities in which South African government officials are involved. And in Holland, gifts up to 1 per cent of individual income are not deductible, but further amounts are deductible up to a maximum of 4 per cent. The working group also found no apparent correlation between the rate of tax and the availability of exemptions; some of the highest rates are accompanied by the lowest exemptions—e.g., Norway, Denmark, and the United Kingdom.

However, a list of European foundations, with no pretense to all-inclusiveness, runs to 9 single-spaced pages. And European interest in the foundation principle is increasing. The conferees concluded, accordingly, that a second working group should be planned, to discuss program rather than legislation. It was decided that the possibility of an information service on European foundations should be explored, and that closer association should certainly be promoted between foundations and the various international cultural associations. Finally, it was agreed that a small task force should be set up to deal with the question of tax incentives.

Part II

FIELDS OF ACTIVITY

The 1963 Grants Picture*

NOTE: The 1964 tabulations did not appear in the original article, and are not included in the discussion. They have been added to the table, however, because they are now available. For the first time grants of smaller foundations are widely represented. The total is substantially larger and some of the proportions are significantly altered.

GRANTS reported in *Foundation News* this past year numbered 2,341 and totaled $324 million, compared to 1,983 and $315 million in 1962. Foundation Library Center judges that if its estimates for total grants in these periods are reasonably accurate, grants recorded represent somewhat less than half the actual flow of funds in the indicated years.

The Center reports only grants about which it can learn (since larger foundations report more fully, our figures may show certain biases) and records only grants of $10,000 or more. Therefore the table below may be considered suggestive but not comprehensive.

Table 1. GRANTS OF $10,000 OR MORE REPORTED IN 1962, 1963, AND 1964, BY MAJOR FIELDS

Fields	*1962*		*1963*		*1964*	
	Amount (millions)	*Per cent of total*	*Amount (millions)*	*Per cent of total*	*Amount (millions)*	*Per cent of total*
Education	$145	46	$ 83	26	$186	33
Health	32	10	35	11	129[a]	23[a]
International Activities	52	17	82	25	74	13
Sciences	45	14	47	14	58	11
Welfare	20	6	24	7	44	8
Humanities	16	5	48	15	39	7
Religion	5	2	5	2	26	5
Total	$315	100	$324	100	$556	100

[a] The 1964 *Health* is disproportionately high because of inclusion of The M. S. Hershey Foundation's gift of $50 million to establish a medical school in Pennsylvania.

Education was once again the most favored field, although both its dollar and percentage lead over other categories declined sharply. It must be remembered, however, that the 1962 Education figure includes a Ford Foundation grant of $27.5 million to the Woodrow Wilson National Fellowship Foundation.

The most startling change in flow of foundation funds is the sharp rise, percentagewise and in dollars, of International Activities. This category for the first time challenges Education for the top position—though not in terms of total dollars that flow into Education, for colleges and universities receive most of the dollars here credited to the challenger. It should be emphasized too that The Ford Foundation is the major factor in this increase in internationally oriented dollars, representing in the 1963 tabulations some $63.8 million or 78 per cent of the total recorded by the Center.

The only other surprising change in the grants picture is the rise to third place of the Humanities, with $48 million and 15 per cent of the total. While there is apparent today a growing concern with humanistic ventures, the 1963 figure is discounted somewhat as a trend indicator by two huge grants, again by Ford—$6.1 million to nine repertory theater companies, and $12.5 million to Lincoln Center.

Grants for the Sciences remained relatively stable and other shifts were small in scope.

The Usefulness of Money

RAYMOND B. FOSDICK*

THERE is a common fallacy—and even some foundation executives may not be immune from it—that money can create ideas, and that a great deal of money can create better ideas. . . . [But] there is no substitute for brains. The difficulty is the lack of men with fertile spirit and imagination, men with basic training or with flaming ideas demanding expression. For them there is no alternative; without them money will purchase nothing but motion and futility.

* From *Chronicle of a Generation* (© 1958 by Raymond B. Fosdick); Mr. Fosdick was formerly President of The Rockefeller Foundation.

Ford and Other Foundations in Public Affairs

DYKE BROWN*

THE FIELD of public affairs remains one of the great "underdeveloped areas" of private philanthropy. Though foundations have contributed generously to education, medicine, and other sectors, they have given relatively little support to governmental and public affairs. A 1957 survey found that while education accounted for 47 per cent, the field of government (including citizenship, city and regional planning, public administration, civil liberties, and the administration of justice) accounted for only 2 per cent of foundation spending.

Why is this so, in view of the key importance of public affairs? Several factors play a role. For one thing, while there are any number of groups campaigning for greater aid to education or health, public affairs has not had the benefit of this sort of advocacy. It has had no champion or "interest group."

Tax—and Other—Problems

Tax considerations also have presented a problem. A certain amount of ambiguity has always surrounded the question of what sort of group may or should receive foundation support. The tax laws give exemption to groups organized and operated exclusively for educational, scientific, or charitable purposes, "no substantial part of the activities of which is carrying on propaganda, or otherwise attempting, to influence legislation." But these terms are quite general and have been subject to considerable variation in both administrative and judicial interpretation.

Furthermore, it is more difficult to channel contributions in the public affairs field. There are fewer qualified, tax-exempt organizations working in this area. There is, for example, no counterpart to the Committee for Economic Development dealing with governmental or political processes. In the area of law and justice the American Law Institute is a notable

* Formerly Vice-President, The Ford Foundation, with responsibility for public affairs programs.

exception, and the American Bar Foundation's program is beginning to get under way. But few organizations corresponding to Kansas City's Community Studies, Inc. or the Stanford Research Institute are to be found in any state or locality.

Moreover, even for groups which are properly tax-exempt, there is always the possibility of controversy—something which many American organizations (especially tax-exempt ones) avoid.

Finally, when a foundation delves into public affairs it often finds itself in the eerie domain where knowledge ends and guesswork begins. In designing a project dealing with juvenile delinquency, for example, a foundation has very little in the way of "hard data" to go on—it must play it by ear. This "fuzziness" has long discouraged foundation trustees. Thus in 1914 Frederick T. Gates, principal adviser in philanthropy to John D. Rockefeller, sought to prevent The Rockefeller Foundation's entry into the social sciences by asking: "Can you command this material as you can command the materials of investigation in medical science? I fear not." Mr. Gates temporarily won the day.

Before World War II

Despite these factors, a few foundations did experiment with public affairs in the period prior to World War II. In the main, their efforts were concerned with research studies at the local level.

The Thomas Skelton Harrison Foundation (established in 1919) provided research funds to look into Philadelphia's municipal courts and its transit problems.

The John Randolph Haynes and Dora Haynes Foundation (established in 1926) supported research into Los Angeles' regional planning problems, and also sponsored studies of the courts.

In 1937 the Samuel S. Fels Fund sponsored the establishment of the Institute of Local and State Government at the University of Pennsylvania, with the aim of encouraging research, training city managers, and providing a consulting service for cities bent on administrative reorganization.

The most active foundation in public affairs before World War II, however, was The Rockefeller Foundation. It attempted to launch a study of labor relations during World War I, but the project quickly died amidst a Congressional investigation. In 1923, however, The Rockefeller Foundation spun off the Laura Spelman Rockefeller Memorial and hired Beardsley Ruml as director. Soon after his appointment Mr. Ruml noted, in a confidential memo: "All who work toward the general end of social welfare are embarrassed by the lack of that knowledge which the social sciences must provide." He promptly launched a series of grants aimed at encouraging university research in the social sciences and recruiting more manpower for these disciplines.

The Spelman Fund (1929–1948), an offshoot of the Memorial, initiated a program which gave special emphasis to public administration. The Fund supported the establishment of the Public Administration Clearing House to coordinate work in this field. It also backed an internship program for young men interested in entering the Federal civil service. Harvard University, American University, and the National Institute of Public Affairs were among the recipients of grants aimed at spurring graduate work in public administration and raising the level of competence of federal administrators.

In the years since World War II a few additional foundations have moved into public affairs—but only a few. Significantly, the new entries have attempted to extend their programs beyond the public administration area and into the more difficult but crucial area of the political process.

The Maurice and Laura Falk Foundation (established in 1929), for example, helped Judge Arthur Vanderbilt establish the Citizenship Clearing House to develop a local, state, and national internship program in practical politics for college students and professors. The Eagleton Foundation has established a program at Rutgers University which brings politicians to the campus to teach students the practical side of citizenship. The Coro Foundation in San Francisco and in Los Angeles supports local internship programs in government as well as other projects aimed at making politics "a laboratory science." The Field Foundation and The New World Foundation have been concerned with race relations and civil rights. And there are, of course, a number of others.

The Ford Foundation

During the past decade The Ford Foundation has had a continuing program in public affairs. In the Trustees' report of September 27, 1950, the Foundation announced its intention to "support activities designed to secure greater allegiance to the basic principles of freedom and democracy in the solution of the insistent problems of an ever changing society."

In its initial stages, the Foundation's Public Affairs Program tended to follow the guidelines laid down before World War II. Grants extended general support to such groups as the National Municipal League, National Civil Service League, Public Administration Clearing House, and other groups striving to upgrade public administration. Meanwhile, a special grant of $15 million set up The Fund for the Republic to operate as an independent organization.

In recent years, however, the Foundation has tended to sharpen its focus and to carve out specific areas of concentration. Its emphasis has shifted from management and public administration to policy and the political process.

One area of concentration is improvement of the public service, in particular through the use of internships. The Public Affairs Program, building on the foundation laid by the Stern Family Fund, has supported the Congressional Fellowship Program in Washington, which gives able young journalists and teachers of political science and law a year's internship with congressmen and senators. Ford Foundation grants have extended the same device to the state level, through funds for legislative internships in twelve states; graduate students in government, journalism, and law spend a year as regular staff members with state legislatures. In New York, internships in Federal agencies have been supported for college seniors, providing actual experience in governmental agencies as a part of college education.

In the field of politics, the Foundation has helped finance pre-legislative conferences in a number of states, participated in by legislators, by nationally-recognized experts in such fields as education, highway construction, and taxation, and by civic leaders, state officials, and members of the press. Among the purposes: to help state legislators obtain more information on complex issues; to focus public and legislative attention on these issues; to stress the importance of "non-political" consideration of common problems; and to upgrade the staff work performed for state legislators.

Also in the political area, the Foundation has supported a special two-week bipartisan conference in Michigan, attended by twenty representatives from the two major political parties. The conference was designed to help the two parties discuss common concerns and upgrade the quality of party workers.

In efforts to help solve the growing problems of American cities, the Foundation has supported a wide range of projects dealing with city government, transportation, education, unemployment, and juvenile delinquency. These projects began with efforts to bring research and scholarship to bear on urban problems. They then moved on to provide help for creating community-wide agencies (in metropolitan Detroit and Philadelphia) embracing all major civic, political, and academic groups. More recently, as Foundation efforts have concentrated on the human and physical problems of slum areas, demonstration grants have been made directly to governmental units such as school systems and city departments.

Action or Research

As The Ford Foundation has sharpened its focus in the field of public affairs, its program has tended to become increasingly action- rather than research-oriented. And where research projects have received support, they have been intimately related to action programs. Greater emphasis has been placed on the concept of the "demonstration project"—a project designed to bring to bear what knowledge there may exist in a given area in the hope of stimulating further experimentation and of expanding this knowledge. This has been particularly true in work on urban problems and juvenile delinquency.

All this, of course, has entailed certain problems. It is manifestly more difficult for a foundation to negotiate a demonstration grant in a community than it is to channel research stipends to scholars. It means taking political risks and it means harder staff work. But if philanthropy limits its role to research, it will realize only a part of its potentialities. Furthermore, a foundation that approaches its public affairs goals with objectivity will find surprisingly few political pitfalls along the way.

The Challenge

One point is clear: philanthropy must increase its effectiveness if it hopes to explore the vast array of critical problems which cry out for support in the public affairs field. Although progress has been made by foundations in public affairs, the surface has barely been scratched. We have scarcely looked into the problem of developing leadership in a democracy; of bridging the gap between our intellectual life and our political life; of evolving new career channels to attract outstanding young people into public service and into the political party machinery; of developing for young people the kind of education and other experiences which will lead them, in the words of Cecil Rhodes, "to esteem the performance of public duties as their highest aim"; of lifting the horizons of children in the slum areas of our cities; of rejuvenating areas of chronic unemployment and poverty; or of intelligently conserving our resources, both urban and rural.

These issues pose a challenge not only for the big national foundations but also for smaller foundations, whose operations are centered in a specific community. A minority of local foundations, such as the Wieboldt Foundation in Chicago, the Rosenberg Foundation in San Francisco, the Mellon funds in Pittsburgh, and others, have long had effective local public affairs programs. In recognition of the important role which such local foundations play, The Ford Foundation has been searching for ways to strengthen local philanthropy and to date has made two grants of $1,250,000 each to the Kansas City Association of Trusts and Foundations, and to the Greater Cleveland Associated Foundation. This is a particularly important trend, for the national foundations are only able to plant their "seed money" in a few communities. Ways must be found in which increasing resources can be applied by local foundations to the pioneering of new approaches within their communities. Only through such locally-directed efforts on a continuing basis can these communities cope with their mounting problems.

"Politics is the practical exercise of the art of self government and somebody must attend to it if we are to have self government," Elihu Root said four decades ago. Clearly, philanthropy has a vital role to play in public affairs and in helping a democracy to understand and solve its problems.

Aid Abroad: Some Principles and Their Latin American Practice

J. G. HARRAR*

IN SEEKING to aid underdeveloped nations through technical collaboration—in agriculture, in other natural sciences, or in the social sciences—there are certain principles which should be kept in mind. For one thing, it is important to distinguish between need and opportunity. Vital human needs are easily recognizable and readily demonstrable in many parts of the world, but real opportunities for foreign agencies to alleviate these needs are not always so clearly defined. Compassion and good will are laudable virtues, but they can become misleading if allowed to blind one to fundamental problems. It is inaccurate as well as tasteless to talk about the application of foreign "know-how" as the complete solution to human requirements, since most commonly demonstrated human needs are not of such simple solution.

Unfortunately, but understandably, too often there is a sense of urgency involved in foreign aid programs, accompanied by heavy pressure to achieve maximum accomplishment in a minimum period of time. But the very facts responsible for lack of development may themselves mitigate against rapid solutions. It is wise to spend both time and thought in preliminary surveys and in evaluating current and long-range problems, as well as their possible solutions. For this, competent individuals must travel widely in the country in question, consult extensively with leaders in all relevant fields, and ascertain the thinking of the political and social leaders of the state. Slowly, critical problems become apparent and what local people would like to have done about them becomes known. Finally, there may be agreement on the over-all type of program to be initiated, the identification of projects of greatest importance, those of collateral emphasis, and details of effective organization.

* President, The Rockefeller Foundation; formerly Director, program in the agricultural sciences; first Director of Mexican Agricultural Program. These remarks have been excerpted from public speeches and articles by Dr. Harrar.

Local Resources

It is important to keep in mind the economic and technical resources of the country receiving foreign aid. No such program should require greater expenditures than the local budget will readily sustain. Neither should it contemplate rapid growth to dimensions that will outstrip the number of available national personnel who can be trained, with the view of ultimately taking over entire responsibility. It is very much better to initiate technical aid projects slowly and permit them to grow only as rapidly as accomplishments dictate. Periodic review, and modification to suit changing conditions, are essential to continued vitality, and the entire project should fit itself into the cultural pattern of the host country. And at some point the effort should become such an integral part of over-all local activities that foreign technical aid is no longer urgently needed; it will then be possible to begin to withdraw, with the assurance that the work will continue and expand under completely national auspices.

Personnel

Technical competence alone is insufficient in the selection of foreign aid personnel. It must be accompanied by an international viewpoint; a determination to learn local language and customs; the ability to see local problems in their logical framework; and the willingness to work within this framework. Recruitment of appropriate personnel is one of the most difficult tasks of technical collaboration in the foreign field. If urgency and expediency are substituted for a careful process of selection, eventual disadvantages will far outweigh any brief and transitory gains.

The greatest contribution any foreign technical aid program can make does not lie in technical accomplishments themselves, but rather in total impact on the recipient nation. People must first become convinced that the program is one of good will and of real value; that foreign operating personnel desire to become a part of the community; that empire-building is not contemplated; and finally, and most important of all, that there is in fact a definite and sustained effort to transfer imported knowledge and skills. Only then will there be general acceptance of the results obtained, and only then will these be applied to the amelioration of local conditions.

Training

The formal and informal training of young nationals is the most vital single factor in this type of program. Admittedly, this must sometimes be started at a very elementary level, often with many delays and discouragements. But every trained national becomes one more person who may devote his life and efforts to the solution of his country's basic problems; the number and competence of such individuals developed by a technical collaboration program will in the long run determine its total success.

There are several ways of helping to train the nationals of the host country. The first and most fundamental is through the strengthening of local institutions. A second method is by training graduates of local institutions within the technical aid program, overlaying their academic experience with practical application to local situations. This process tends to focus attention upon national requirements; it also carries over into any training these men may receive abroad, since they begin with better knowledge both of their country's problems and some of the possible solutions. A third training technique is the use of external fellowships or scholarships, and an essential fourth method involves the strategic utilization of such persons after their return from abroad. Helping to place trained nationals in positions of usefulness is of maximum future benefit. And this alone is not enough: it is often necessary to continue to aid these young scientists both morally and materially, helping them to become established, to direct or to carry out locally significant projects and programs, and to aid in the training of subsequent generations.

All four techniques have been utilized in The Rockefeller Foundation's collaborative agricultural programs with the governments of Mexico, Colombia, and Chile.

Mexico

The agricultural operating program of The Rockefeller Foundation has its beginnings in a 1941 request for technical assistance from the Government of Mexico. After preliminary stages of study, orientation, and selection of projects, a small group of American scientists of proven ability and accomplishment was brought together in Mexico, the several individuals to serve as nuclei for the development of basic sectors. By mutual agreement, these men initiated interlocking projects aimed at the improvement, both in quantity and quality, of basic food crops, attacking all those factors of greatest importance in limiting yield. Each of these men was surrounded by a group of young Mexican agricultural graduates, who acted as both colleagues and trainees. All the work was carried out on a completely cooperative basis: the entire operation was organized as a semiofficial office of the Ministry of Agriculture. The young trainees participated in every phase of the research, from the most elementary to the final step. Many of those with special aptitudes were subsequently granted Foundation scholarships for further training abroad; others entered directly into various phases of agricultural science and production. They were then replaced by younger men, and the cycle continued. Almost 250 have thus far been enabled to complete advanced degrees abroad; over 600 have had practical in-service experience.

Most recently, the establishment of a National Institute of Agricultural Research has served to consolidate the program with other Ministry of Agriculture research units. It also places major responsibility for technical and administrative matters in the hands of Mexican scientists. And a locally based graduate school has been created: advanced training can now be obtained in Mexico, and in Spanish. As the graduate school expands it can be expected to assume regional and then hemispheric significance.

Colombia and Chile

As the program in Mexico developed, other countries became interested in this type of collaboration. In 1950, together with the Ministry of Agriculture of Colombia, the Foundation set up a second cooperative agricultural research program. This has now grown to substantial proportions—and one of its most gratifying aspects has been the demonstration that the improved materials produced, after years of intensive research, in the Mexican program, were immediately useful in other areas with similar climatological conditions. The background experience gained in Mexico has made possible much more rapid progress in some areas of Colombia. And the still newer program, established in Chile in 1955, has been able to profit from the accumulated data of both the earlier efforts.

Information and improved materials produced in all three countries have been distributed widely and exchanged wherever it appeared they might be useful. The exchange of visits by agricultural scientists representing the several Latin American countries has been encouraged, and important international scientific meetings have been sponsored. Moreover, more than 75 young scientists from some 10 other countries of Latin America have received in-service training, principally in Mexico. These men, on their return, have assumed posts of high responsibility.

The Inter-American Food Crop Improvement Program (formally initiated in 1959) is still in the embryonic state. At first concerned with maize, and then with wheat, it has now been expanded to include attention to potato improvement. This new type of hemisphere-wide program seems likely to help maximize the effectiveness of Foundation staff and funds.

Summary

Friendly nations cannot resolve the fundamental problems of the less developed or emerging nations, but they can help to speed the processes of social and economic growth by collaborating in projects of readily demonstrable benefit that can be completed or ultimately transferred to local agencies. Intensive preliminary planning of such projects, and careful selection of the personnel assigned to them, are essential to success. The most basic consideration of all, however, is the extent to which each project can serve as a training facility for the nationals of the countries concerned. Only by emphasizing the training aspect of foreign assistance is it possible to develop permanent roots and to achieve continuity and multiple benefits from an enlarging force of competent personnel able to serve national needs.

Support for Social Research

DONALD YOUNG*

IN THE AMERICAN TRADITION foundations, like institutions of higher learning, welfare agencies, and other benevolent organizations, are administered by trustees and officers who, with few but notable exceptions, can only be described as amateurs in the accomplishment of the objectives of such organizations. Foundations of course have problems of management involving matters of law, investment, or public relations which make it highly desirable that these fields be represented on the board of directors. It is taken for granted that directors with these skills will participate fully in the consideration of all proposals. They must nevertheless be regarded as amateurs, albeit amateurs of integrity and good judgment, when decisions must be made on technical matters of health, welfare, education, or research, and need the aid of colleagues proficient in their foundations' areas of operation.

Primary dependence of foundations on trustees who are public-spirited citizens of good ability and repute has assured high purpose and a generally high level of managerial integrity. It is a pattern of management which worked especially well in the less complex days when it was established, and still can work well when a foundation operates in a relatively small community or has a comparatively simple task, such as the distribution of its income to well-known agencies for their established programs. On the other hand, the disregard of many modern broad-purpose foundations operating in our involved urban society for specificity in trustee knowledge and experience has permitted the development and persistence of excessive anti-intellectualism in concern with social affairs, dependence on superficial information in decision making, and self-imposed isolation in operation. Note that it is said that these traits are excessively prevalent, not that they are all-pervading.

Foundation Anti-Intellectualism

Anti-intellectualism may be thought too strong a term to use in referring to foundations' general practice of plunging ahead with projects and pro-

* Visiting Professor, The Rockefeller Institute, formerly President, Russell Sage Foundation. These remarks have been adapted from "Philanthropic Foundations, Sociology, and Human Betterment," an address before the 1962 meetings of the American Sociological Association.

grams of social amelioration with little or no regard for preparatory research or later evaluative review. Certainly their major emphasis on education and on research in the physical and biological sciences is evidence that they are strongly proacademic in matters concerning the material world and life itself. In contrast, attack on the problems of social living, of people getting along together in communities, in nations, and in a world made up of troubled nations, commonly is thought to require action without the delay and expense incident to rigorous study. Also, it is humanly more interesting and rewarding to deal directly with people's woes than to study their origin and nature in the hope that the resulting knowledge will lead to improved ameliorative and preventive measures.

Acceptance by foundation managers of the popular view that social questions are best answered by common sense and a warm heart encourages dependence for proposals, and advice in decision making, on like-minded individuals. Friendship and compatible bias afford personal reassurance in deciding whose advice to seek and what proposal to support when adequate technical knowledge is lacking. Furthermore, it is far from easy for the layman to obtain dependable advice on the relative utility—for his purposes—of the various social disciplines, or on the comparative merits of individual social scientists. There is common confusion concerning the relative advantages and limitations of sociology, social psychology, social anthropology, geography, political science, and economics for improved understanding of a given social problem. The distinction between social research and social practice also is rarely clear; there have been and will continue to be many foundation grants for social research to be carried out by social workers and psychiatrists with training and experience primarily in practice.

The Problems of Privacy

Western culture's respect for individual privacy limits receptivity to the research approach in human affairs. The intimate story of an individual's life and troubles is conceded to be pretty much his own affair, if no law is broken, and preferably kept to himself unless he is a public figure. The notion persists that, ideally, social problems are best solved by those who have them and next best by kindly relatives and neighbors or volunteer citizens. In other words, although concern for individual welfare is a social virtue, action growing out of such concern should in the minds of many avoid the appearance of an invasion of privacy—a difficult accomplishment if social research is to be utilized.

Philanthropy, too, is a private matter in the American ethos. True, the legal privilege accorded foundations of escaping the two allegedly inescapable eventualities, death and taxes, assumes acceptance of the principle that as public trusts they are subject to the requirement of ultimate public accountability. Nevertheless, the tradition of attributing special virtue to privacy in benevolence, and the concept of individual freedom in disposal of private property, have helped keep social research a minor factor in foundation social benefactions. Emphasis on privacy argues against the use of social science analysis in foundation programs and projects, and imposes no need for evaluation of accomplishment. Furthermore, the socially approved desire for privacy perhaps has been the dominant factor in the persistence of a policy of isolation of foundations from each other in operation. This policy of not learning from each other's experience is defended as a means for assuring independent objective appraisals of proposals so that one rejection may not lead to others; to the extent that it is valid at all, the argument is a confession of weakness. The socially granted privilege of giving for the benefit of others through the instrumentality of a foundation carries with it the obligation to give wisely on the basis of a full knowledge of relevant circumstances and modern investigative techniques, a principle incompatible with secrecy and isolation in foundation giving.

Taking Risks, Breaking Ground

Foundations avoid controversy like the plague. Granted that no one seeks criticism and attack in the performance of an intended good deed, there is reason to fear public disapproval of support for social research and action in areas of strong citizen sentiment. Fundamental in this avoidance pattern is the understandably prevailing attitude that social stability is good and that the burden of proof is on those who urge that some modification of existing patterns and values is desirable or even worthy of consideration. This is a sharp challenge to those who consider foundation funds "venture capital" or "risk money." In fact, proportionately very little foundation money is expended as "risk money." The bulk is invested in "blue chip" agencies and projects where there is little chance of public controversy and criticism, very nearly as it would be invested if expended directly by those who made or inherited it.

The fact that all but a small fraction of foundation grants are made to well-established agencies, and for relatively standard activities likely to be well received by press, legislature, and the general public is not mentioned here as criticism. In so expending their funds foundations are serving the main function for which they have been granted privileged status by society. It is an important function—if only because the resulting diversity of support and direction of scientific, educational, and charitable efforts is needed to help avoid stultifying homogeneity in management and operation. And, continuously, there is a small but significant stream of foundation money flowing into venturesome projects in controversial areas. Those who regret that this stream is not much larger may ask themselves how much it might be increased before social disapproval were to bring about restrictive action.

Centralized Competition

The foundations must inevitably expand their activity in social research, training, and application, in consequence of the path-breaking example set by the federal government. It has long been said that foundations have the advantage of freedom to pioneer with projects far too controversial or uncertain of results for support by tax money under political control. This has been important in the past and may be important again in the future, but does not seem so at present. Foundations have yielded leadership in such controversial areas as race relations, medical care, care of the economically and socially disadvantaged, prevention of unemployment and poverty, mental health, and others. In the physical and biological sciences the government is taking as great risks as any foundation ever did. In the social sciences the federal government is far in advance of the foundations in basic research, training, and application, not just in the number of dollars expended but, more importantly, also in dependence on professional peers of applicants in the selection of projects, institutions, and individuals for support, in the breadth of subject matter and method accepted for consideration, and in willingness to accept the fact that many projects must fail in order that the unpredictable one of significance may not be missed.

Trends and Prospects

A promising development, in recent years, is to be found in advances in management in a small but expanding number of foundations of all types, including small family foundations as well as large general purpose foundations, community funds, and company-sponsored foundations. There seems to be a little less distaste for "institutionalization" and more acknowledgment that the reason human activities are so widely institutionalized is that nstitutionalization is a superior way of supplying continuing needs. Secrecy in operation is becoming more and more a matter for apology and explanation not in terms of privilege but of the need to avoid a mass of appeals out of proportion to assets and facilities. Isolation is giving way to an open desire to learn from the experience of other foundations. Perhaps the clearest evidence of improving management is the growth of inter-foundation conferences, such as the annual Conference of Southwest Foundations (since 1949), the annual meetings of the National Council on Community Foundations (since 1950), the New York University Biennial Conference on Charitable Funds (since 1953), the informal monthly, except summers, meetings of the Foundations Luncheon Group in New York, and several others held at least twice in Minnesota, Michigan, and California. Characteristically informal as these conferences are, they nevertheless reflect an appreciation of the fact that foundation operation cannot remain a casual, personal matter, and that it really may be true, as Julius Rosenwald observed many years ago, that it is more difficult wisely to dispose of than to make a million dollars—at least for some people.

Support for Humanities

W. McNEIL LOWRY*

AT ITS MOST BASIC LEVEL, art is not about money, or facilities, or social acceptance; it is about the surge of artistic drive and moral determination in the individual artist or artistic director. It is, of course, true that these forces can improve the quality of life in this technological age. But we can never measure that quality by quantitative means, no matter how many buildings nor even how much money our technological society may come to devote to cultural affairs. . . .

Foundations, like other sources of funds for the arts, could choose to act only from motives that are finally irrelevant to creativity or the creative artist—the educational motive, for example, or the broadly social motive. Indeed, it must be said that foundations historically have shown much more adeptness at these motives for actions in the cultural field than at others.

What I am about to propose, however, is that of all the potential patrons of the arts—individual, corporate, or public—foundations have the best opportunity to act from a professional motive in the arts, as more central to artistic considerations than the other motives I have discussed. How does one act from the professional motive? By accepting the artist and the arts on their own terms. This does not appear to be a very unorthodox requirement when we consider how easily (in the main) philanthropy accepts, say, scientists or educators on their own terms. Philanthropy in the arts is professionally motivated only when it learns from the artist himself at least to *recognize* the atmosphere in which the artistic process is carried out, intruding itself into the midst of a fraternity with the same fanaticism and abnegation that are that fraternity's hallmarks.

It has been my privilege for six and one-half years to help carry out such an exploration for The Ford Foundation. Whether it is music, theater, painting, creative writing, ballet, or opera with which we are concerned, we talk to many artists and artistic directors in the field and attempt to gain a realistic insight into the problems with which the artist is confronted. Through our extensive fieldwork in every part of the country, through un-

* Vice-President, The Ford Foundation; formerly Director of Humanities and the Arts. Excerpted from "The Foundation and the Arts," an address delivered 11 November 1963 at the Manhattan School of Music.

publicized conferences and panels in New York, through interviews with individual men and women in our offices, we *listen.* Anything we know about the arts we do not read from books nor attempt to view from our own vantage point in New York City. We are catalysts rather than reformers, participants rather than backers, communicants rather than critics. And when we announce a specific program for individual artists, both the nominating and the selecting processes are in the hands of the artists and artistic directors themselves.

Unlike corporations, government authorities, and even most individual patrons, we have the opportunity to work in this way because we have no other work to do. It would be a severe dereliction in our duty if we said our subject were only philanthropy and not its objects, which in our part of the Foundation are the humanities and the arts. We know that money cannot create a painting or write a musical score or train an artist or produce a play. Recognizing our own role, therefore, we spend the greatest part of our time trying to understand the role of the artist or the artistic director in the many fields in which we are active. We relate people and information, in short, and so continuous is the link between us and the artists with whom we deal that our existence serves as a communications network for the artists themselves.

With the arts as an ethic or an esthetic taking on a new doctrinal urgency in this country, the role of a foundation willing to accept the artist on his own terms can be both challenging and influential. Along the way it may even set some few benchmarks by which government and business may develop their own philanthropic activities in these fields.

New Ideas for Cities as Learned from Foundation Grants

PAUL N. YLVISAKER*

I AM OFTEN ASKED whether all the millions foundations have spent under the label of improving urban community life have yielded important results. In answer, I would say the accomplishments of foundations have been considerable.

Former Pittsburgh mayor, David Lawrence, and his successors in City Hall, could tell you what part the Falk and Buhl foundations, and the several Mellon funds, have played in that city's renaissance. Mayor Naftalin could tell you about Louis W. and Maud Hill Family Foundation in the life of Minneapolis-St. Paul and the Northwest. Mayors Clark, Dilworth, and Tate could tell you what it has meant to have Samuel S. Fels Fund providing research, training, and consultant help in Philadelphia. New York still owes much to Russell Sage Foundation, which was the financial name behind the New York Regional Plan in the 1920's—the "granddaddy" and model for the regional planning movement in the United States. And no listing would be complete without including the many examples of enlightened corporate and community foundations.

But I am also frank to say I do not think the potential of philanthropy in contributing to the solution of community problems—especially urban community problems—has been more than barely realized. There are a number of reasons.

One is social lag. Just as generals too often find themselves fighting the last war, foundation trustees frequently find themselves engaged with yesterday's problems. The community archaeology is retraced in each successive round of annual giving. Hostages are given to concerns of the past until the foundation's annual report and so-called free funds freeze into ancient history. For a mayor to get risk money from such a foundation for work on new problems would mean fighting a David and Goliath battle with the past. I wouldn't blame him if in many cases he decided the battle wasn't worth the effort.

* Director, Public Affairs Program, The Ford Foundation. This material is adapted from an address before the American Municipal Congress in Houston, Texas, 12 August 1963.

Another reason is hidden in the first. The areas where mayors and communities most need foundation help are also likely to be the hottest spots in the municipal kitchen. Our cities could use some help breaking through obsolete building codes; finding paths through the political minefields of tax policy; experimenting with new patterns in race and labor relations; developing cures and preventive medicines for municipal corruption; devising new approaches in local-state-federal relations; improving living environments and transportation systems; exploring alternatives to the present systems of welfare and relief; etc., etc. But these are tough issues, and whoever tackles them has got to be ready to live with controversy and uncertainty every step along the way. Not strange that many a foundation would choose some easier or more familiar fields in which to work—not strange, but given the potential and purpose of philanthropy, most regrettable.

A third reason—again related to the others—is that foundations and municipalities have tended to live in separate worlds. The former dwell mostly in the world of education, research, charity, and the "long run;" the latter in the world of action, policy, social bargaining and the here-and-now.

It is my own conviction—as well as that of The Ford Foundation and a fast-growing number of other foundations—that our urban community problems and the potential of philanthropy are both too great to let past reason govern future behavior. With so much at stake, and so much to offer, philanthropy will have to start doing business with City Hall.

Ford Foundation Efforts

This brings me to The Ford Foundation's work with urban problems, most of which comes under the Public Affairs program. Beginning about six years ago, the trustees decided to concentrate Public Affairs staff work and grants on the problems of our rapidly growing and decaying urban communities. Since 1957, 130 grants totalling $30 million (and more in commitments) have been made under the explicit label of "Urban and Regional Affairs." An almost equal number of grants, totalling $13 million, have been directed at problems of juvenile delinquency and youth developments—almost all of them concerned with urban areas. And in each of our other Public Affairs categories, the urban emphasis predominates. For example, our grants in law have concentrated on problems of legal aid and defense, especially among the low-income groups of the central city.

As far as subjects are concerned, we have covered the urban waterfront. Grants have been made for work on these problems, among others: police administration; urban renewal; metropolitan government; housing; planning; taxation and finance; transportation; education; civil defense; zoning; public works technology; minority groups; migration; man-power and training; voting and apportionment; research; and even municipal corruption. Our approach in making these grants has varied. In some cases, our money has gone to universities. In others it has gone to individuals, professional associations, leagues of municipalities, church groups, and not least, to municipal corporations.

Municipal Partnership

What have we learned from our experiences? First, the longer we have been active in urban affairs, the more we have been inclined and encouraged to make our grants within range of the municipal firing line. In earlier years, we concentrated heavily on research and on the community of scholars. This helped us to get our own bearings, to separate real problems from pet notions, to set priorities, and to find the places where action could best be started.

We haven't abandoned research. But we have shifted considerably toward projects which involve action and experimentation, and which bring us into a working partnership—or dialogue—with those responsible for making and executing public policy.

We have also tried to establish working relationships with local foundations, hoping to get the combined benefits of our somewhat greater resources and possibly wider perspective, certainly of their greater local know-how and continuing interest. In Boston, New Haven, Washington, and Pittsburgh, various projects are jointly financed by Ford and local foundations. In Kansas City and Cleveland, the idea of combining or otherwise coordinating local trusts and foundations so as to maximize their resources and potential has taken hold; and as evidence of its interest in this idea, The Ford Foundation has made block grants to these associated foundations for them to devote, as they see fit, to the solution of community problems.

As another operating trend, we have relied more and more on the advice and guidance of men experienced in urban affairs. Recent additions to our staff have included the former Commissioner of the Federal Housing Administration and the former chief of research of the New York City planning and housing agencies. We have also relied increasingly on the consulting help of mayors and other municipal officials.

Grants and Ideas

Now what of some of the ideas that have emerged from Ford Foundation grants, or have precipitated them? Here are some examples drawn from three different series of grants during the last five years.

1. *Urban Extension:* Several years ago, we realized that this increasingly urban nation had not yet developed a system of support for our cities and suburbs comparable to the network of research, education, and extension services which for a century had been available to agriculture. We had made a number of grants to encourage urban research and training in selected universities, but these efforts were bits and pieces which tended to get lost in the vastness of the job at hand. So we wondered whether, if the hundredth anniversary of the Morrill Act (which in 1862 had established the system of land-grant colleges) were to be "celebrated" by launching a set of analogous urban research training and extension programs, the nation might not catch the hint and do for its cities what it had earlier, and most successfully, done for its farms.

Grants were shortly made to ten institutions and the experiment was on: Rutgers first, then Wisconsin; Delaware; Purdue; Illinois; Oklahoma; California; Missouri; the National 4-H Club Foundation; and Action-Housing of Pittsburgh, cooperating with Pennsylvania State University, Duquesne, Pittsburgh University, and Carnegie Institute of Technology. The size and specifics of each grant varied. What they had in common was a declaration of intent to take a fresh look at urban community problems and to see what help, if any, the universities could be in alleviating them.

So far, about $3 million is riding on this experiment. Being somewhat bankerish, we took the precaution of establishing a committee to review and evaluate the results—not afterwards, but while the experiments were going on. Mayors William Hartsfield of Atlanta, Frank Zeidler of Milwaukee, and Arthur Naftalin of Minneapolis, agreed to serve along with James Pope, retired editor of the Louisville *Courier-Journal.*

There have been some false starts, wasted motion, differences of opinion, and the usual frictions between departments within the university. In many ways, the analogy between agricultural extension and urban extension breaks down and no one is yet certain there can be such an animal as an "urban agent." But Mayor Hartsfield, long the skeptic, says he has finally found a "real one" in at least two of the projects. And there are a growing number of other encouraging signs. Through the anguishing moments of change and involvement, the universities are beginning to realize the healthy impact of learning while doing, in the exciting arena of knowledge which the urban community represents. And local officials are beginning to appreciate the continuous backstopping which a university can provide.

2. *The City as People:* The Ford Foundation has made a number of grants involving considerable sums to analyze and improve the physical plant and economic base of our urban communities. But cities are first of all people; and we have tried to place first things first. Our largest urban

grants and our major attention have been given to experiment with new ways of improving the social conditions of the central city and of opening new opportunities to those now living in these urban "gray areas."

There have been two stages of grants relating to human resource development. The first pointed to the schools in the deteriorating parts of the central city. They were designed to test the following ideas:

1) that an investment in the schools of an urban gray area—if the choice has to be made, and in many cases it does—would have a greater pay-off in arresting the decay of the city than an equivalent amount spent on bricks and mortar for the central business district;

2) that new and effective ways can be found to break through the cultural and other barriers which have inhibited good teaching and learning among the newcoming minority groups in the central city, and new ways of breaking out of the educational and opportunity trap in which these newcoming groups too often find themselves.

This first series of grants was made to the school systems of Buffalo, Chicago, Cleveland, Detroit, Milwaukee, Philadelphia, Pittsburgh, San Francisco, St. Louis, and Washington, D. C. The results have not yet been thoroughly evaluated, but what we have seen so far more than justifies the funds and energies which have gone into the experiment.

It was the intent of our second round of grants to see whether schools and City Hall, and for that matter all the community's relevant agencies—public and private—might find common cause and common policy relating to development of human resources in the "gray areas." For a long time, while we were searching the land for communities willing to tackle the idea, we were inclined to think we were permanently in no-man's land. For there are not many communities willing to take on frontally and explicitly the tough and different jobs involved: of trying to mesh the policies and operations of separate public and private jurisdictions; of working with minority groups, and particularly the Negro community; of looking beyond old and fixed ways of doing things, to invent new approaches in education, housing, welfare, and the rest.

But some forward-looking and intrepid communities did emerge, and in the last two years we have made substantial grants (each about $2 million) in Oakland, New Haven, Boston, and Philadelphia, to establish what are, in effect, "research and development" laboratories directed at improving the conditions and opportunities of minority and low-income groups in the central city.

It is too early to judge the results of these projects, but already fresh winds are stirring. Oakland has pioneered some highly effective techniques in inter-agency cooperation. New Haven has found ways of relating the schools to urban renewal and neighborhood services, and has come up with a job training program which has already been given national recognition. The kinds of commitments these projects represent, the facilities they provide for developing and testing ideas, and their organizational advantages have begun to attract the interest and resources of other public and private bodies, including demonstration grants from a variety of federal agencies.

3. *Manpower and Executive Development:* A common thread of thinking and strategy runs through the many and diverse grants we have made. We believe that the strength and survival of our nation, and the other nations of the world, depend increasingly on the health and vitality of our cities and metropolitan areas. In our grants for "urban extension," and the city's forgotten people, we have been trying basically to help create the back-stopping facilities our urban communities need to come of age, and to discharge the responsibility for major policy development which modern society has thrust upon them.

It was in this mood that a few years ago, The Ford Foundation and the American Municipal Association joined in helping to organize the Municipal Manpower Commission, headed first by James Webb, and after Mr. Webb's appointment as Administrator of the National Aeronautics and Space Agency, by John Corson. The Commission has completed its work. The most important of its conclusions, I think, was its statement that we have emerged from the "negative" period of thinking about municipal personnel—a negative attitude which had been expressed and perhaps had too long survived among some of our Civil Service commissions—and are now at the point where positive measures are necessary. Not merely is this essential in recruiting the thousands of specialists which we are short of in nearly every field you can name; not merely in paying them what they deserve and encouraging them to move freely from one jurisdiction and level to another. But it is important because it recognizes the needs and requirements which are implicit in the office of the mayor, as the symbol and instrument of modern community leadership. The municipal personnel system should find its logic in what society demands of its chief executive, and its standards should be performance.

The notion is a powerful one. Its time has come and it will take more than tinkering to give it form and substance. But take form it will. I would not be surprised to find mayors in 1973 given personnel systems and staff facilities rivaling those of major corporate enterprises in the United States: flexible pay plans; research and development laboratories; executive training systems; and, who knows, perhaps even an improved public image.

In ten years, we will need all this. And if we are going to have it, and viable urban communities, we had better get cracking.

The Role of Foundations in Community Affairs

HOMER C. WADSWORTH*

Is THERE A DISTINCTIVE ROLE that a foundation can play in community affairs that would not otherwise be performed by a social service agency, a unit of government, or a college or university? This is a basic question, for if a substantial case is not possible, the future of community foundations is uncertain indeed.

One may frame the problem from various standpoints. A general distribution of foundation funds to legitimate charities and educational institutions is hardly objectionable, though it is all too readily apparent that the amounts of money involved are of minor importance in the aggregate. Our experience in Kansas City in recent years is fairly typical. Our member trusts have been spending about $450,000 per year—an amount less than one per cent of the total community bill for health and welfare services alone, and apart from patient charges for medical and dental services. If your community is twice the size of Kansas City—a metropolitan area of about one million persons—you may simply double our expenditures and measure them against the aggregate of foundation contributions to arrive at a comparable percentage. The result will be sufficiently accurate to make the point stick: foundations working at community levels contribute in a very modest way to the underwriting of our major community services.

The Community Foundation

This analysis of matters brings into high relief the fundamental problem of the community foundation (or trust)—that is, the community foundation with broad discretion in the use of its resources. (For the community foundation with pre-allocated funds problems of a different sort are involved.) How may such a group serve best the total interest of a community and all of its people, rather than special segments thereof? This appears to me possible only as we construct appropriate ways of assessing our total commu-

* Executive Director, Kansas City Association of Trusts and Foundations.

nity conditions—its facilities for human services of all kinds, and the persons engaged in providing these services—as a basis for determining the particular kinds of things peculiarly suited to support for varying time periods. This is to regard foundation funds as essentially venture capital, and with a general charge to use such money in ways quite comparable to the function of risk capital in business and industry.

Two observations are perhaps necessary at this point. The first is that the American community is caught in a web of difficulties arising from a more rapid *rate* of cultural change than at any previous period in history. The growth of our population, the mobility of our people, the urbanization of the nation, the technological revolution in both business and agriculture—these are the driving forces that create conditions for which our instruments for planning community services are largely inadequate. A further complication arises from the general reluctance of all established institutions to make the adjustments necessary to cope with changing conditions—the inertia in human affairs that preserves both the desirable and the undesirable, the sound and the unsound, in policy and practice.

A good illustration may be drawn from the field of social service. The structure of these services has been built in layers over the years. Each generation adds its own, usually in response to new knowledge or technique, without giving much thought to the effect upon existing services. Since the main sources of support are either voluntary contributions or governmental payments, the programs involved are framed in public relations terms—i.e., in ways calculated to win legislative approval or to extract contributors' dollars. This approach has the unhappy tendency of obscuring important facts, and skews the distribution of money in strange and often indefensible ways. The results are all too apparent: a rather disorderly array of services, largely uncoordinated, ranging in quality from very good to very poor—often in the same community.

If this diagnosis of our general condition is correct, what then are the special areas deserving foundation attention at this time? Three such areas come especially to mind: social and cultural research; experimental effort to improve our facilities for community and regional planning of services in health, welfare, and education; and improvement of means to communicate knowledge to the general public.

Each of these facets of community life is remarkably weak at this time. The knowledge upon which our community services is based is very thin in spots, just as current practice in many cases is divorced from such knowledge as we do possess. Moreover, no suitable connection exists between the students of our society and those who minister to its ills—the kind of connection that has transformed teaching, research, and patient care in medicine in the past fifty years. Most of our great universities have faculty members in the social sciences far more knowledgeable about social affairs abroad than in the communities of which they are a part.

Planned Planning

A similar weakness is apparent in community planning. Our present instruments were created to meet the requirements of federated voluntary agencies. They do not in most cases embrace the whole of the metropolitan areas of which they are a part. Neither do they take due account of the fact that the main burden financially, both in education and in the social services, is now assumed by various governmental agencies. Planning implies systematic effort to anticipate problems and to construct suitable ways of avoiding critical conditions. It is at this point that our present machinery is least effective.

Public decisions are likely to be only as good as the information on which they are based. This places large responsibilities on political leaders to provide the necessary facts and to stimulate public discussion. This has become rather difficult to do, and notably as government has plunged into more and more areas, requiring a considerable effort by the citizen to understand the complexities of the issues involved. This is really a communications problem at many levels, for the expert in a specialized area is frequently as badly informed as anyone else in subject fields apart from his interest.

Local Venture Capital

Community foundations enter this picture with highly useful ingredients. While their funds are not large as measured against the aggregate of expenditures, they are free to commit or not commit as the circumstances warrant. It is an unhappy fact that most communities and most service agencies and educational centers have great difficulty in finding free money—that is, funds not vested by the terms of legislative action or budgeted on the basis of past experience. Consequently, the availability of foundation funds encourages new thought, experimental activity, and sensitivity to changing conditions. The really significant grant is one that encourages creative and imaginative people to feel that there is support available for their efforts, recognition in the doing, and active interest in creating a milieu favorable to the research point of view. This is an important part of a foundation task—subtle in nature, complex in application, and yet indispensable to community progress.

Community foundations give much more than money. They give solid and tangible status—to persons and agencies and institutions—that is frequently of greater value in the long run than the immediate cash payments. In part, this is because foundation trustees customarily enjoy positions of responsibility in business and professional life, and their service is usually without tangible compensation. Moreover, they are sufficiently close to local affairs—especially if staff work for them is done competently—to act in related matters with better knowledge of conditions than would otherwise be likely. This has special importance in view of the need to develop mixed financing, involving often both governmental agencies and private parties, so as to mount programs on the scale necessary to deal with many complex problems.

Inter-foundation Cooperation

One of the areas largely unexplored is the manner in which foundations should relate to one another. Their purposes are similar, except where special conditions restrict trustees, whether they serve national, regional, or local interests. Community foundations properly organized have intimate knowledge of local conditions and people, and bring both financial and moral support to approved programs. The national foundations, on the other hand, have impressive resources, tend to know the national scene well, especially the university world, but have limited means for exploring the great variety of circumstances in a nation so diverse as ours.

Two lines of experiment seem to me possible in this regard: (1) federation of community foundation interests to use available local funds as wisely as possible; and (2) development of appropriate means of interchange of information and judgment between foundation personnel at various levels, with responsibility for grant supervision placed wherever it can best be managed. These efforts are calculated to improve foundation service to the broad public interest, which is the heart of our purpose and our reason for being.

The foregoing suggests some of the elements which make up the role of a community foundation and its officers. As Dr. Weaver so wisely indicates,[1] foundation people must be good listeners. They must avoid involvement in partisan matters, though they must be fully conscious of the importance and, indeed, the necessity of spirited public debate. They must build a network of viable relationships with those who bear the heavy responsibilities of directing various community activities, according to each the respect and sympathy each deserves. They must seek to create a public understanding of what foundations do and do not do, based largely on performance rather than published statements.

[1] See pp. 66, 68.

Foundations and Religion

G. HAROLD DULING*

ALTHOUGH MANY small foundations list religion as one of their chartered purposes, there is a paucity of major national foundations with such stated grant-making interest. One might appropriately ask, "Why have the foundations steered away from religion?" Do they wish to avoid controversial issues? Is it timidity? This seems improbable, for, throughout their history, foundations have given to the social sciences, which are at least as controversial as religion. The almost complete secularization of philanthropy in the United States is something of a paradox in a Christian democracy.

Even so, the Lilly Endowment has not found religion an easy field in which to operate. In a pluralistic society, with its wide variety of religious traditions, how is one to decide where money can be wisely placed and effectively used? Which of the many church and interdenominational agencies are most worthy of assistance? What kinds of research are most promising in this field? Suppose one were trying to place a grant which would reach all of the "old-line" denominations, to say nothing of other confessional or faith groups. What sponsorship embraces all of these? There is no body that is broadly representative of American religion. The Lilly Endowment has attempted to aid a few projects with collective sponsorship which have turned out satisfactorily. But before foundation assistance can be used effectively by religious enterprises, we need to learn a great deal more about ecumenical financing and interdenominational and interfaith co-operation.

Because the extent of foundation gifts in this field is small, such giving serves as little more than "pump-priming" as compared with gifts received directly by the churches from their own members. Even so, a church history professor wrote us recently to express "a slightly negative observation on possible foundation influence on religion." He went on to say, "I'm afraid that the foundations may, by their necessary involvement in wealth and American patriotism, encourage unduly a shallow culture religion of superficial personal adjustment and mutual congratulation, with extremely phari-

* Deceased, 1964. Formerly Executive Director, Lilly Endowment, Inc. This material is condensed from the Endowment's 1958 *Annual Report*.

saical and unhealthy results." We share the professor's premonition in all but his original premise. With a comparatively small amount of money available for grants in the field of religion, foundations will hardly become a determinative influence.

Foundations may be able to support projects which have not excited the interest of established boards or which have been neglected by them. The foundation has a freedom which is lacking in many institutionalized church organizations because of pressures from the denominations. Since the foundation operates from the outside, it may be able to see the situation in religion in a way not available to those who must largely follow established patterns.

Money can never be more than a catalytic agent which brings about progress as envisioned by wiser leaders in a field. The way to accomplishment in religion is varied, but we can be sure that the strength of the Christian Church will depend largely on the religious faith laid in childhood in Christian homes and on such support as we can draw from our Christian and Jewish heritage.

Part III

VIEWS ON ADMINISTRATION

Thoughts on Philanthropy and Philanthropoids

WARREN WEAVER*

SHOULD A FOUNDATION have a program? In the early days of The Rockefeller Foundation there was an imaginative and vigorous Trustee who used to say, "Our policy should be to have no policy." And there are circumstances under which this free-wheeling and flexible notion will work, times when no policy is in fact the best policy. But there are basic differences in this regard, I think, between large and small foundations.

It seems to me that a large foundation is almost obliged to have a defined and clearly stated program. This should of course not be immutable; on the other hand, neither should it shift and change, on the occasion of each individual decision, with the flexibility which can more properly characterize a smaller foundation.

A large foundation is far more in the public eye: not only do newspapers and the general public watch and wait for its actions, but the less numerous public of grant-seekers watches too. Accordingly, where a large foundation cannot (or thinks it cannot) take up a fair number of closely related alternatives, all equally worthy of support, it is not justified in taking up just one such, unless of course there is a strong case for aiding a single "pilot project" to demonstrate the potentialities of all the other similar ones.

Put in a different way, a large foundation cannot afford to look at the vast array of all projects through a small hole in a large piece of paper—a hole through which one can observe the attraction of that single project, without seeing the competing attraction of the others. Seen in that way a proposal can seem very wonderful indeed, wholly unique, immensely attractive. And the man proposing it can seem capable of wonders. But a large foundation simply cannot approach projects in this way. It is obliged to think wholesale—to look for the other holes in that same piece of paper. How many are there? Do they represent a total field of activity that the

* Vice-President, Alfred P. Sloan Foundation; formerly Vice-President, The Rockefeller Foundation. These remarks are summarized from an address before the Foundations Luncheon Group in New York City, 11 January 1962.

foundation can, or should, or wants to get into? Is there any reason—strategic, social, intellectual, or moral—for preferring the opportunity seen through this one particular hole to all the others of about equal merit and urgency? Unless the large foundation is prepared to deal with more than just the one isolated instance, it must usually decline the invitation. Indeed, unless a project is evaluated by comparison with its natural alternatives, it is not objectively evaluated at all.

No foundation, of course, can work in all the possible fields where its money might be spent. No foundation is large enough to be able to afford such an attempt, and a small foundation certainly cannot even contemplate it. For the wise spending of money requires a great deal of knowledge, coupled one hopes with a reasonable amount of wisdom. The acquisition of knowledge is a costly process, both in time and in money. You have to be prepared to talk to a great many people, asking questions and then listening, hard and long, to the answers you are given. And the acquisition of wisdom is much more difficult.

Smaller Foundations

I do not mean to imply that small foundations do not require knowledge and wisdom, but I do think that they can properly be more elastic in their choices. Indeed, as far as I can see, they are bound by circumstances to be somewhat more personal or intuitive: for they simply cannot afford a sizeable number of highly trained specialists, traveling widely and keeping intimately in touch with the developing fronts of scholarship so that their decisions can be made on so objective and logical a basis.

The smaller foundations thus are almost forced to reflect, more than a large foundation properly can, the special and personal interests of the founders and the usually rather small staff of officers. I think this is justifiable, and I think it works out pretty well, primarily because there are so *many* small foundations, with such a wide variety of interests and enthusiasms, so that, taking them all together, they do reasonably well and fairly spread themselves over all the opportunities.

I think a small foundation can perfectly properly make a grant to—let us say—a small liberal arts college in which it has a personally-based interest. If twenty other similar small liberal arts colleges come knocking on their door (the door of their safe, presumably) the small foundation can simply say, "We made the grant to Little Ivy simply because we have a special interest in them, but we are not prepared—and indeed are obviously not able—to consider similar grants to a lot of similar fine small colleges."

A big foundation, with national or even international scope to its program, and with wide and eagerly sought publicity for all its grants, just cannot make that kind of reply. I shall return to this subject in a moment. Let me first say something about the person who is to accumulate and make use of this wisdom, the foundation staff member or officer—the philanthropoid. He characteristically comes to his job with little or no specific preparation. I'm not sure there can be any very sensible pre-training aimed specifically at making a good foundation officer. It is a little like a parachute jump. All the talk and the reading and the preliminary exercises don't do much more than get you up there, more or less willing to jump. Then you close your eyes, swallow hard, and "hit the silk." Having survived one test, you proceed to the next—and the next—and the next. Perhaps there should be, but as far as I know there are no courses in how to be a philanthropoid.

Philanthropoids: Some Requirements

On the other hand, I find that many of my friends feel that the job must be a *very* easy one. What it amounts to, after all, is getting rid of money, and they have no trouble at all in getting rid of theirs. But giving away money *wisely* is quite another thing. It is an extraordinarily subtle and difficult task, with moral, social, and intellectual complications that keep your conscience active and your mind bothered. There are so many kinds of people who quite legitimately need help, and so many ways of going about helping them. The philanthropoid needs intelligence, imagination, flexibility, and a large streak of unselfishness. Interesting yourself in other people's goals and ambitions is essential; there are people who cannot do it. There are also people who *can*, and who find publicly unobservable, perhaps forever hidden pleasure and satisfaction in knowing that they have helped. A good philanthropoid must be one of this latter breed.

The good philanthropoid must have a real zest and talent for understanding and dealing with people. And this zest and enthusiasm simply *must* be tempered by that undefinable something called taste. The philanthropoid sits on one side of the desk, the applicant sits on the other. Money, and all that goes with it, sit beside the philanthropoid. These are funds, further, to which he has clear responsibilities. But while he guards the foundation's resources he must also be able to enter into the thoughts and the aspirations of the person on the other side of the desk; he must be able, in a very delicate and sensitive way, to sit on both sides of the desk at once.

This is not to say that he must in any way *direct* the people who come to him for help. Sometimes there is a temptation to clink and clank the money bags a little, meanwhile expressing regret that the visitor is interested in the wrong things. "Now, if you had happened to be interested in . . . ," you might say, clanking the coins a little harder in your bottomless purse.

And then perhaps the applicant will perilously think that he is indeed interested in what you happen to be interested in and would like to support.

That is a very dangerous situation; it can degenerate badly, and become disgraceful both intellectually and morally. The philanthropoid must *never* tell anyone what he ought to be interested in. As I said before, he must ask questions and *listen to answers.* He must not plant the answers he would like to have coming back to him. He, of all persons, must never start a question by saying, "Don't you think . . ."

Locating the Most Worthy

Not all the people to whom the philanthropoid talks are seekers of funds. One of the most serious problems confronting any foundation, large or small, is evaluation of fund-seekers, determination of who is good, and therefore worthy of support, and who is not good, and therefore not as worthy of support. There are two principal ways of establishing such matters—and neither of them depends to any very significant degree on pieces of paper. You never learn such things from pieces of paper, recommendation forms or any other. And you have to be very skeptical about standard "recommendations." If you ask a potential source of information whether or not Mr. Jones or Miss Smith is a first-class prospect, you will almost always get "Yes" as most of your answer.

No. The two methods which seem to me productive are first, to accumulate a body of slowly acquired information, patiently built up over many hours of careful questioning and even more careful listening by very competent and trained officers; and second (more suitable in the case of smaller foundations), to have an informal body of advisors to whom one can go directly with special questions. The first method, which involves a great deal of traveling about, a large staff, and a lot of time and patience, is clearly available only to a rather large foundation, in part because it is a much more costly approach, in part because it is a much slower one. Large foundations usually do not try to move as rapidly as their smaller brethren. Or this first method may be used, within a fairly narrow field of activity, by a foundation of moderate size. But in both cases it is less productive to ask for information about specific people. You ask, instead, who your informant thinks "are the better young people," the up and coming people, in his special field. To a question like this he will generally reply with relaxed ease and accuracy—and once you have visited enough eminent men, and collated the lists obtained from them, you will have a pretty good idea of who is and who is not first-rate in that particular subject. Certain names will come up over and over.

You can also ask such informants, or the first-rate prospects to whom they point, what they are interested in doing that (for a variety of reasons) they cannot now do. This is a fruitful source of suggestions; it avoids the basic curse of putting proposals into an applicant's mouth, and at the same time it may help define the otherwise unsupported, perhaps only dreamed-of areas into which excellent people would move if they only could. I must add, with respect to the smaller foundation and its group of informal advisors, that for each such man or woman there must also be a correction factor, an adjustment which can be made to allow for the inevitable biases and crotchets of the human mind. A really good and experienced philanthropoid is an expert advisor concerning advisors. Any foundation which relies on uncorrected advice is asking for the trouble it will undoubtedly get.

Another function which such questioning serves is the encouragement of variety in giving. This is extremely important: the multiplicity of interests shown, in particular, by the smaller foundations seems to me a wonderful thing. If all foundations, of whatever size, began to act in the same way it would be disastrous. I am very much in favor of the National Science Foundation. It provides important support, and its budget is a big one. But if it ever acquires anything like a monopoly on support for research in the sciences, at that moment I will be against it. The variety that exists in our democracy from Maine to Texas, from Florida to Oregon, seems to me the way a democracy must and should operate. Smaller foundations have a right and a duty to be themselves. Larger foundations, in fact, are sometimes too timid, and back away from things in fright. It sometimes takes very little to frighten a large foundation. The proposal is a fine one, the job ought to be done, but then they start asking themselves how many more parts to the job there are—and can they possibly support all of them? Certainly not, and so they shake their heads and sometimes do nothing. Smaller foundations need not hesitate in this way. They should say, "It is interesting, it is important, and we are going to do it." And then it gets done.

Rejections

Foundations must of course be allowed to turn down proposals. There is a good deal of talk about their being public institutions, especially once they have obtained tax exemption—as though this meant that the public then should decide who gets the support. Foundations do assist many people, and in a broad sense their funds are public, but private persons created the organization, gave it direction and instructions and officers to carry them out. These men cannot be deprived of the responsibility and the right to decide how and when the moneys entrusted to them will be spent. There is no law which has said they are to abdicate in favor of anyone else.

Their decisions must be within the general limitations of their charter, and must not offend the law. The rest is up to them.

When they turn down proposals, further, philanthropoids have to be sure that their rejection is cast in perfectly spherical, polished form, with no protuberances that can be grabbed hold of so that the declination can be thrown back at them for explanation or reconsideration. If you make the serious mistake of pointing out a flaw in the proposal, the applicant will write to you, some months later, with the glad tidings that this flaw has now been corrected, thanks to your wise advice—and will you please send the check by return mail? Sometimes declinations presume to say that the field or the problem in question itself is not important enough, but this is dangerous and usually untrue and, in any case, who has the wisdom and foresight to make such judgments? Not foundation officers! Nor can you tell the rejected applicant what is almost invariably the real reason for your decision, namely, the cruel and humiliating fact that the man is just not good enough.

Finally, let me say something about the intellectual lives of foundation officers—philanthropoids all. Some time or other the trustees of foundations have to learn that money which they label "overhead," or "administration" (and try to reduce to minimal proportions) is in reality not a business cost at all, but an investment fully as important as the other investments in people which they authorize with no similar qualms. Philanthropoids must have intellectual lives of their own—and if their trustees do not think so, or are unwilling to invest in the intellectual lives of the officers they have, they ought to get themselves some new officers. They are not safe with the ones they have. Philanthropoids need not be expert in a wide variety of fields, they need not be the world's most eminent scholars of this and that and the other thing, but they must stay intellectually alert. How else could they possibly sense opportunities, and test them, and understand them? And how else can they earn, and keep, the respect of all the people on whom they, and their trustees, and the public too, so clearly depend?

What the New Foundation Executive Should Know

JAMES A. PERKINS*

I DON'T THINK it is really possible to advise a new foundation officer: he must create his own universe. I have helped to break in a good many younger officers in the Carnegie Corporation and I can remember very well what the man who hired me, Charles Dollard, said when I first arrived: "In the end every foundation officer must be his own foundation."

I do however have six things I want to say which may or may not be useful to a neophyte foundation officer. And each of these six points is, in turn, a series of propositions that must be formulated in balanced pairs. For in the end, the art of management—be it a foundation, government bureau, or business enterprise—really involves the skillful business of dealing with what seem to be antithetic, balancing, even contradictory forces.

1. Freedom and Control

A foundation has to work between two very powerful imperatives—freedom in the public interest, and public supervision in the public interest. The foundation is, under the first heading, part of the private world with which we and all free and pluralistic societies are familiar. It operates outside the direct control of government, and is frequently protected from direct or even indirect control by public authority itself. It is supposed to be spending most of its time, energy, and certainly most or all of its money on matters in the private domain. Its board is supposed to be free from outside control. Its officers, subject to board authority, are in turn supposed to operate in the private domain and, typically, to work with other philanthropic enterprises.

The other side of this coin, however, is that in most cases foundations are also agencies created by some public act, either a state charter or occa-

* President, Cornell University; formerly Vice-President, Carnegie Corporation of New York. Mr. Perkins' remarks are adapted from an address before New York University's Sixth Biennial Conference on Charitable Foundations; a full text has been published, in the Conference *Proceedings*.

sionally a federal charter, subject to the scrutiny of the state authorities who have issued the charter and subject to the scrutiny of those who have a responsibility for seeing that the tax exemption enjoyed by these private agencies is being justified by their activities. At one and the same time, therefore, we have an agency dedicated to the concept that it is important to have free institutions preoccupying themselves with the public welfare, but an agency in a sense publicly regulated and continually to be supervised in terms of its actual devotion to the public interest.

Foundations have been through a series of public discussions as to what this appropriate balance is and I would say to the new foundation officer that he should become intimately acquainted with the Congressional investigations of the 1950's, the first headed by Representative Cox of Georgia, the next by Congressman Reece, and the current one by Congressman Patman. There is also the increased interest of federal agencies, particularly the Internal Revenue Service. These are very important investigations, in good part because they illuminate the way in which our society is grappling with the complexities involved in living with these two imperatives.

The new foundation officer will note that most foundations feel these two forces can best be balanced through what we call the function of complete disclosure. Full reporting, full disclosure of assets, full disclosure of grants made, full disclosure of purposes and activities, are the great public regulators that foundations are more and more coming to use to present their case to the public: that they are indeed operating with both freedom and the public interest in mind.

2. Leadership and Leverage

A second balancing set of considerations lies between influence on the one hand and minority status on the other. It is a fact that, within the fields where they operate, foundations do exercise an enormous amount of leadership and influence on persons, institutions, and ideas. And this comes about even though the money they represent is only a fraction of the total philanthropic dollar and the philanthropic dollar may be only a fraction of the total number of dollars operative in the field.

There are I think three reasons for this. First, foundation money is uncommitted. By that I mean that typically foundations do not commit money, if they are wise, for years in advance. I remember somebody telling me that the difference between Harvard and Carnegie Corporation was that Harvard has five hundred millions of endowment and Carnegie Corporation only two hundred-fifty millions. But the fact of the matter, it was pointed out, is that Carnegie has an enormous advantage: it has all assets and few liabilities.

Second, all foundations—or at least the best among the larger ones—have highly professional staffs, people who are fully competent in the fields in which their foundations operate. This is a relatively new idea, perhaps forty or fifty years old. Before that foundations were considered the charitable impulse of their donors who, buttressed by a few friends, would give money to people who presented themselves. This relatively recent professionalization provides foundations with as much leverage as does the first factor—their uncommitted money.

Third, foundations are able to deal with the *causes* of problems. They are not bound, as many other institutions are, to deal with *effects*. And this means that foundations can operate one-half step away from the heat of immediate problems with which other organizations, and particularly public organizations, must deal.

3. Too Soon or Too Late

A third dichotomy (and this is not so much a dichotomy as a balancing of considerations): a foundation must learn to have a sense of timing. On the one hand it has to be very careful that it does not give its money too soon, but neither should it dawdle over a request. I have yet to hear anyone complain that a foundation made a grant too soon, at least not a recipient. But we get a lot of complaints about foundations not acting soon enough.

Mr. Keppel, who was president of Carnegie Corporation, once summed it up very well by saying that a really good grant represents a conjunction of the stars. That is, it is an idea brought forward by the right man from the right institution *and* at the right time. I frequently use the Midwest Inter-Library Center as an example. Mr. Hutchins came to the Corporation with this idea and told us that he just wanted to lodge it in our mind, that he would be back when he thought the time was ripe. Back he came. But he waited eleven years until he thought the institutions and the libraries in the midwest were ready.

If you give a grant too soon you can sometimes drown a field with money, or you can assist the wrong people, or right but unprepared people. To use another bit of foundationese, you can burn over a field by bad timing and litter the area with a kind of aroma of unsuccess.

4. Shotgun vs. Rifle

You have to know how far to concentrate in a field in which you are operating, and on the other hand what kind of obeisance to give to the opposite doctrine of flexibility. The literature is full of absolutely conclusive cases for both policies. The case for concentration is both a familiar and a good one: if you don't work within an area where your money can be effective you will lose it, you won't know whether or not you are doing anything important. You will be subject to "scatteration," a word that came up vigorously in the Cox investigation.

There are other difficulties if you don't concentrate. You begin to lose your board of trustees and your public. I would say that the foundations which have operated most effectively have been those which have kept their board and their officers and their public in step with each other. And the foundations able to do this are those that have managed to concentrate their grants in fields at least narrow enough or concise enough so that a board has some idea of what its staff is up to. It is a very tough business being a responsible trustee in a foundation. Projects come up individually, they don't all come up in any consistent bunch. You may be dealing with a topic that comes up in three different board meetings during a year and it takes a very agile board member to make sure he understands that you are following some kind of logical program. If your board members cannot predict what you are going to do they will have no confidence when you come up with a request, and if they have no confidence in their officers, the officers have to be far too timid in dealing with their clients. If an officer has to say too often, "Well, I haven't the faintest idea of whether there's a chance of your getting this grant until the trustees look at it," then pretty soon you can be sure that clients will be looking in your little booklet to find out who the trustees are, because there is no advantage in dealing with staff who merely act as mailboxes for their trustees.

On the other hand, flexibility is a matter of very great importance. Foundations that announce with great rigor the areas in which they work, that are very precise as to how they are going to spend their money and consistently turn people away because, by some very narrow margin, the grant doesn't fit into program, are also in danger. Even foundations that have developed a conclusive case for concentrating their grants into very specific fields should always have an escape valve. Maybe you ought to have a category called "miscellaneous" or "unexpected." But in my judgment no good foundation should ever be without some administrative elbow room for dealing with a very interesting idea or a very important man, even though neither meets the tests of concentration. Of course, to play everything by ear, by the next man who comes in, is to get into all the difficulties I mentioned earlier. So the good foundation officer will keep in mind the necessity for picking fields of operation that are commensurate with the capabilities of staff, with its size and its origins, on the other hand keeping enough elbow room for dealing with the unusual chances that come along. They should, perhaps, be kept unusual but they should never be eliminated.

5. Active and Passive

The new foundation officer will pretty soon begin to wonder what his particular role in life is. On the one hand, he will be told—and indeed it will be true—that he should be neutral. He should not continually throw his own ideas around too heavily, too often, and certainly not too soon. There is a general feeling that a foundation officer ought not to be continually trying to sell something. He ought to be more on the receiving end than on the giving end, at least as far as ideas are concerned.

On the other side, it is argued that foundation money is precious money, seed corn, or venture capital. And the function of a foundation officer under this theory is to develop new ideas, to push them hard and even push them in areas where the people concerned do not like them.

Obviously, between these two pictures of the foundation officer—the neutral man, or the aggressive foundation officer who is trying to think of new and original ideas on which his money can be spent—there is a necessary balance. Let me suggest some of the things that will facilitate its development.

The business of listening is almost the number one function of a new officer. And this is very hard for some of us. It is particularly hard for the young man off an academic campus who has been teaching for a few years, who has found that it was his function to talk while it was the function of the students to listen. To get into an office where he is to spend minutes and hours listening and listening and listening is very important but very hard. And you have no idea how much of a difference it makes in the client-foundation officer relationship if the man who comes into your office feels that he really can get out of his mind what he wants to say and is not bumping up against a man who is merely holding back his own speech.

The second thing that will keep you in some kind of balance between neutrality and aggressiveness is the necessity for continually checking and rechecking your judgment of the people with whom you deal and, equally important, your judgment about the people whose advice you take about the people with whom you deal. You must always check the judgments of your network.

I would say that the most critical advice I could give to a new foundation officer is the importance of having your own network of advice. As a matter of fact, I don't think any foundation officer is any better than the particular network of advice that he has, and the extent to which he knows how to count on it. The foundation officer is operating at his best when he is just a bit ahead of the best people in the field, when he knows who the best people are, when he has been able to develop a judgment about them and is therefore able to push on into this area ideas which represent a validly-formed judgment.

6. Professional or Human?

Lastly, there is the balance between the importance of one's official responsibilities and one's professional relationship to the client and the importance of human understanding. Here again, the extremes have trapped many foundation officers, operating under correct but incomplete premises.

One premise is that foundation giving must be a professional business, that you must deal with clients without reference to the fact that they happen to be friends of yours. You must develop, under this theory, not a cold, but a completely professional relationship. The function of giving and receiving money ought never to sound like charity. And all this is true, but it isn't enough.

The other extreme runs like this: when you are dealing with money you have to recognize the fact that you have a very sensitive relationship with your clients. You must unfreeze the coldness that comes from dealing with money; it is important that you begin to recognize the human qualities involved in the person with whom you are dealing.

In my judgment both these statements are correct. The neophyte foundation officer must be able to push his friends off if they use their friendship as the key to his vaults. He must also, however, cut through the business of handling dollars so that he can have a correct but still a warm and human relationship with the people with whom he deals. Otherwise, as I have found, you can be led astray about people every single day of the week.

Tax Exemption and the U.S. Treasury

DEAN RUSK*

NOW, FOR THOSE who are worried still about this notion of exemption of charitable institutions' own funds, let me [say] . . . that in my judgment the impact of these exemptions has been greatly exaggerated. You can take, for example, the federal income tax. Does it really make any difference that the federal income tax is imposed upon, say, colleges and universities? I would think not, because when colleges and universities get through in the course of the year in doing the only business for which they are chartered most of them, so far as I know, do not have any income. Annual deficits are not a very profitable source for levying income taxes.

Even in the case of a foundation such as ours, when we get through doing in the course of a year the only business for our being, which is philanthropy, we have no income tax. We have no income.

But suppose . . . we were taxed like any ordinary business corporation. We would start with a large deduction on the 90 per cent of our income which comes from the dividends we receive from other corporations—something on the order of 85 per cent deduction on the 90 per cent of our income, roughly speaking. We have some business overhead. I think you would agree that we would be entitled to a 5 per cent deduction for charitable contributions. The result is we would owe a very limited amount at best, or worst if you like, as federal income tax, and we normally give several times that amount to activities in which the federal government itself has some vital interest.

Thus the exemption of the treasuries of the charitable institutions is not a matter of any real dollar concern to the federal treasury. They are not living out of the public trough. They are not diverting funds which otherwise might readily go into the federal treasury, say for income tax purposes. This is particularly clear when one realizes that these capital funds in colleges, universities, foundations, and so forth, are not withdrawn from tax-yielding enterprise in the way in which the church establishments at the time of Henry VIII were withdrawn. These funds are invested in productive

* Secretary of State; formerly President of The Rockefeller Foundation, in *The Role of the Foundation in American Life*, lectures delivered at Claremont University College, 1961. © Claremont University College, 1961; The Foundation Library Center, 1962.

enterprise which in turn pays very substantial taxes into the public treasury. The out-payment which . . . a foundation makes goes immediately back into the tax-yielding stream in the purchases of equipment and supplies, the payment of salaries, the payment of transportation, et cetera, et cetera.

My broad point is that economically, and from a policy point of view, this is not a critical and urgent problem for the public treasury.

The Legal Problem of Accumulation

ROBERT H. MULREANY*

THE ACCUMULATION of income[1] by foundations or other charitable, educational, scientific or religious organizations has always presented potential legal problems, under the local laws governing such organizations. Prior to 1950, however, the federal Internal Revenue Code contained no prohibitions against the accumulation of income. In that year substantial changes affecting tax-exempt organizations were made in the Code as a result of congressional investigations which had disclosed abuses of exempt status and overreaching by some tax-exempt entities.[2] The investigations had also shown that some exempt organizations had not been active in carrying out their stated purposes and had been accumulating income without any need or purpose related to their exempt functions. A proposal in favor of a direct tax on all accumulated investment income, not paid out within two and a half months after the close of the taxable year in which the income was received, was rejected in favor of a provision denying exemption in years when accumulation of income was ". . . unreasonable in amount or duration in order to carry out the charitable, educational, or other purpose or function constituting the basis for exemption . . ."[3]

Neither section 504 of the present Code, nor its predecessor, section 3814 of the revised 1939 Code, contains any definition of what is considered an "unreasonable accumulation" of income either in amount or in duration. Official regulations promulgated under these sections are of no aid in de-

* Senior partner of DeForest Elder & Mulreany, New York City. Mr. Mulreany is counsel for The Foundation Library Center and for a number of philanthropic foundations.

[1] As used herein, the term "income" means ordinary income—i.e., it does not include capital gains. See I.R.C. 1954 Regulations Section 1.504-1 (c). However, where exemption is denied for any year, the net of capital gains and losses for that year is subject to tax.

[2] See the legislative history of the Revenue Act of 1950 in 2 *U.S. Code Congressional Service*, pp. 3078 to 3092; 3163 to 3187; 3239 to 3246.

[3] Section 3814, I.R.C. 1939, as revised 1950; now section 504, I.R.C. 1954. *Cf also* section 681, I.R.C. 1954, which applies a similar restriction to charitable trusts. This provision does not apply to qualified educational institutions having faculties and conducting schools, to religious organizations, or to hospitals and medical and agricultural research organizations. See section 504, I.R.C. 1954, and section 503(b), I.R.C. 1954.

termining what the test shall be, since these regulations are merely a rephrasing and restatement of the language of the Code itself.

The only guide lines which are available are to be found in Revenue Rulings, containing decisions of the Internal Revenue Service, and in the decisions of the courts which have been obliged to construe the law.

Revenue Rulings

Although some twelve years have passed since accumulation was proscribed, only four published rulings have been issued by the Service and only eight cases have been decided. A ninth case, involving The Danforth Foundation, is now before the courts and an early decision is anticipated. It should be noted that the rulings referred to are published rulings. These are decisions of the Service which are printed and made available to the public and have some reliability as precedents, at least until they are specifically revoked or modified. We are aware that there have been many special rulings of the Service, but it should be pointed out that these special rulings have no value as precedents and cannot be relied upon except by the organization receiving the ruling.

Turning to the published rulings, we find that they may be broken down as follows: two of the rulings permitted a recoupment of capital through partial accumulation over a period of time;[4] one of these rulings also permitted accumulation during a three-year period to allow the foundation to prepare itself for a new venture, but with the restriction that any accumulated income not used to restore capital during the period of accumulation must be spent promptly following the end of the last year.[5] A third ruling permitted accumulation in the sense of transferring to a reserve account commitments of income made in one year which would be expended over a period of three years.[6] The fourth ruling did not actually relate to accumulation per se but held that contributions received during the year were, in general, to be considered additions to capital, and expenditures made during the year for exempt purposes were first chargeable against income received during the year, and only thereafter could they be charged as a depletion of capital.[7]

The rulings have furnished a few general rubrics. They do not however spell out or even vaguely define the thinking of the Internal Revenue Service as to what would be considered an unreasonable accumulation in

[4] Rev. Rul. 54–137 (1954-1 *Cum. Bul.* 289); Rev. Rul. 54–227 (1954-1 *Cum Bul.* 291).
[5] Rev. Rul. 54–137.
[6] Rev. Rul. 55–674 (1955-2 *Cum. Bul.* 264).
[7] Rev. Rul. 58–535 (1958-2 *Cum. Bul.* 270).

amount or duration. For this purpose, it is necessary to turn to the cases which have been decided under this section. These cases serve to indicate the thinking of the Service as to what in their view constitutes an unreasonable accumulation, as well as to provide the judicial canons of construction which will serve as reliable guides in the future.

Court Decisions

The leading case in this area is *Samuel Friedland Foundation v. U.S.*[8] There, the foundation had been accumulating income for the purpose of funding the construction of a medical research building at Brandeis University. The court formulated a test which has since been followed and applied in other cases, saying: "*Does the charitable organization have a concrete program for the accumulation of income which will be devoted to a charitable purpose and, in the light of existing circumstances, is the program a reasonable one?*" The court held that the foundation did have such a program and that the government's denial of exemption due to accumulation was invalid. (It should be noted that the test in *Friedland* bears a striking similarity to the common law tests in force in many states, governing the accumulation of income by charitable or philanthropic organizations.)

In *Hulman Foundation v. U.S.*[9] the court, in line with the *Friedland* case, permitted the accumulation of income for the purpose of constructing a civic building for the city of Terre Haute, Indiana.

Parallel questions were presented in *Tell Foundation v. Wood*,[10] and *A. Shiffman et al.*[11] In both cases the foundations had received real property (i.e., land and/or buildings) as a gift from their founders. The equities in the properties were subject to large mortgages. The foundations had used virtually all of their net income to reduce these mortgages. In both cases the courts held that the income could be used to pay off the indebtedness and that this would not be considered an unreasonable accumulation of income, since once the property was owned free and clear the entire net income would then be available for the charitable functions of the foundations. In both of these cases the real property constituted the sole asset of the foundation.

Truscott v. U.S.[12] held that income could be accumulated for a retirement fund for the employees of a company in which the grantor's family, but not the grantor, had a substantial interest.

[8] 144 F. Supp. 74 (D.N.J. 1956).
[9] 62-2 U.S.T.C., paragraph 9656 (S.D. Ind. 1962).
[10] 58-1 U.S.T.C., paragraph 9111 (D. Arizona 1959).
[11] 32 T.C. 1073 (1959).
[12] 58-1 U.S.T.C., paragraph 9515 (E.D. Pa. 1958).

Davis et al. v. U.S.[13] held that an accumulation of 5% of the annual income of a foundation was not unreasonable inasmuch as the foundation had distributed 95% of its income during the year in question.

Erie Endowment v. U.S.[14] involved an inter vivos trust which had been established in 1935. Under the terms of this trust instrument, accumulation was mandatory until the aggregate accumulations reached $10,000,000. There was no specified program formulated for this foundation. The court held this accumulation to be unreasonable, relying upon the test laid down in the *Friedland* case, above.

Stevens Brothers Foundation v. Commissioner[15] presented several issues, one of them being unreasonable accumulation. The foundation had been accumulating substantially all of its income over a period of some 15 years. When challenged, it claimed that it was its intent to accumulate income until its assets reached the one million dollar mark, at which time it would begin to pay out income. The reason given for this accumulation was that substantial capital was necessary for the foundation's effective functioning. No evidence was presented as to when this goal was formulated, and no evidence was presented as to a definite philanthropic aim or aims of the foundation, in the sense of a concrete program. As in the *Erie* case, the court here relied on the test laid down in *Friedland* and held the accumulation to be unreasonable.

Danforth

The Danforth Foundation case, which is now pending, is an action arising from a denial by the Internal Revenue Service of tax-exempt status for the years 1951 and 1952, due to alleged improper accumulation. During the years in question, The Danforth Foundation made a partial accumulation of income during a transitional phase in which the foundation was developing a program of activity under a new director.

In many respects the decision in the Danforth case will have more importance than previous decisions, since in all of the prior cases "unreasonable accumulation" represented only one of several issues before the court, and in at least one of those cases, *Davis et al. v. U.S.*, the denial of exemption due to a 5% accumulation was an obvious make-weight. Danforth however presents squarely, as its principal issue, the denial of exemption for unreasonable accumulation.

[13] 201 F. Supp. 92 (S.D. Ohio 1961).
[14] 202 F. Supp. 580 (W.D. Pa. 1961).
[15] 39 T.C. 93.

Traps and Perils

On reflection it is clear that the prohibition against accumulation has created a potential morass for foundations where none had existed in years past. Only a few safe landmarks are visible in this legal fen. Thus we know that a foundation may accumulate a small portion of its income to recoup capital which has been expended for grants in prior years, but we do not know whether a foundation may accumulate income to replace a capital shrinkage due to losses or inflation.

We are also aware that the Internal Revenue Service has ruled that a foundation may charge against current income the total amount of commitments payable over a three year period. However, we do not know whether this ruling would also apply to challenge (or conditional) grants, where the conditions do not have to be met in the year when the grant is made and where such challenge is not in fact met within that year.

Again, we know that in the case of a small foundation whose sole asset consists of donated real property subject to a mortgage, substantially all of the net income may be used to pay off the mortgage. What we do not know is whether a foundation could divert income received from other assets for the purpose of paying off a mortgage on property received as a gift or purchased by the foundation as an investment. Would such a siphoning off of income be considered a prohibited accumulation?

Considered in broad perspective, the problem of accumulation under the Internal Revenue Code really presents this dilemma: if a foundation wishes to accumulate income for a purpose which is not identical with the facts of the published rulings or decided cases, then it must make one of two choices. The first is to apply to the Internal Revenue Service for a ruling on the proposed accumulation. The second is to make an independent decision that the accumulation is reasonable in amount and in duration, and to run the risk of denial of exemption. Under the first method, the foundation is in effect forced to take in the Internal Revenue Service as a partner in its decisions. In the second case, it runs the risk of losing its exemption for the year or years in which the Internal Revenue Service considers there has been an unreasonable accumulation and faces the concomitant necessity of paying taxes at the regular corporate rates.[16]

Although the rulings and the cases furnish certain landmarks, they present a trap for the unwary. Thus one would ordinarily assume that there would be no objection to a foundation accumulating income over a period of years to build a medical research building, and turning over the accumu-

[16] Section 6501 I.R.C. 1954 sets the statute of limitations during which the I.R.S. may deny exemption at 3 years from the date of filing the appropriate information return for the year in question, but see *Stevens Brothers Foundation v. Comm.*, above, for the problem of accumulations prior to 1954.

lation in one lump sum, since the foundation could in any case pay over its annual income to the medical school with the provision that it be earmarked as a building fund for the same medical research building. In the latter case no problem would exist, since funds which were income in the hands of the foundation would be capital in the hands of the college. Such accumulation was permitted in the *Friedland* and *Hulman* cases, but only after the matter had been litigated. The uninitiated might also assume that since the Internal Revenue Service had ruled that a foundation could accumulate income for a three-year period in order to properly prepare a program of distribution, and that it had permitted another foundation to take full credit in the first year for commitments payable over three years, that it would permit a foundation to accumulate income during a transitional phase as in the case of The Danforth Foundation and yet such is not the case.

Certainly, present circumstances indicate that extreme caution should be exercised by charitable foundations and trusts in accumulating income.

The Company-Sponsored Foundation

REMBRANDT C. HILLER, JR.*

MANY PEOPLE who recognize the corporation's impact as an economic force do not fully understand that it is also assuming a significant, emerging role as a social institution. Company-sponsored foundations—themselves relatively new and distinct—are an important expression of this role. However, these foundations are for the most part extensions of the contributions programs of the companies which sponsor them: the task cannot be here attempted, but the place of these foundations in our free society should not be considered completely apart from the overall giving program of their creators (who may of course be non-corporate partnerships). And that overall giving has increased, it should be noted, from $30 million in 1936, to $214 million in 1946, to $418 million in 1956, and probably to nearly $500 million in 1961.

Even a cursory examination of company-sponsored foundations reveals a wide range of purposes and objectives. One end of the spectrum is typified by the International Harvester Foundation, which makes about 92 per cent of the combined contributions for itself and its sponsor company and which gives to a variety of charitable, educational, and technical organizations. At the other extreme are special-purpose foundations with very narrow but intensive focus, exemplified by the Bulova Foundation, which trains handicapped veterans for jobs in the watch-making industry.

Advantages and Disadvantages

A survey of 141 companies having general-purpose foundations, reported in 1955 by the National Industrial Conference Board, summarizes the basic advantages and disadvantages, from the sponsoring companies' point of view, of giving through a foundation. The chief advantages noted were favorable tax treatment, particularly for gifts of appreciated securities or other property; stability of giving, despite instability in company earnings; better planning, particularly with regard to longer-term commitments; and greater efficiency, sometimes simply because of centralized ad-

* Vice-President, The Sears-Roebuck Foundation, Chicago, Illinois.

ministration. One foundation noted a much more objective analysis of appeals.

Chief disadvantages were a certain loss of control over the funds; the difficulties of securing and retaining tax-exempt status; lessened participation by local management—the local nature of certain causes sometimes making direct contributions by company units preferable; the necessity of maintaining company memberships, and continuing donations closely tied to company interests; increased requests for giving (but wider opportunities and wiser giving, too); stockholder objections (a diminishing phenomenon, over the last six years); and heavy claims on the time of company personnel.

Basic Facts

Approximately three-fourths of company-sponsored foundations have been established since 1950, with the peak rate of formation coming in the excess-profits-tax years of 1952 and 1953. The selective listing of foundations in *The Foundation Directory, Edition 1,* includes 1,333 sponsored by companies, or a little over one-fourth of the 5,202 total. A study of the Chicago area, summarized in Leo J. Shapiro's *Company Giving,* reveals that in 1956, among companies with 1,000 or more employees, 39 per cent had foundations. (The proportion among all companies, regardless of size, was 5 per cent). A recent N.I.C.B. study, mostly of larger companies, shows a proportion of 46 per cent with foundations. The Chicago study further indicated that company-sponsored foundations were more likely in manufacturing, finance, or communications than in retailing, wholesaling, or service industries.

One interesting and significant fact is that, although gifts made through company foundations tend to be more in number, greater in amount, and broader in scope than would be the case if the company made all contributions directly, company foundations seldom have a large corpus. This is true even for many of the largest-spending foundations, such as the Esso Education, Shell Companies, and International Harvester foundations.

Another significant characteristic is the very high ratio of grants to total expenditures: practically all companies absorb the operating costs of their foundations—salaries, travel, rent, equipment. Most foundation personnel also have responsibilities in the company organization, thus wearing two hats. But even when the executive director and his staff are assigned full-time to the foundation, the company traditionally pays their salaries and expenses.

Of still greater interest and significance is the matter of control. With few exceptions, the governing boards of company foundations are composed of officers or directors of the sponsoring company. Only a handful have seen fit to employ special personnel or invite outsiders to become directors, though there is considerable merit in having at least one outside, or *public*, member on the governing board. In addition to the value of an objective viewpoint, such a public member may be selected in order to bring to foundation decision-making special knowledge in some important field.

Trend to Education

There is a striking trend among companies to direct a greater proportion of their total giving to education, and company-sponsored foundations have been a strong factor in this development. In the Chicago study (*Company Giving*) over 25 per cent of the respondents said that their companies would not have contributed to education, prior to 1957, if they had not already created their foundations. In a recent informal survey of 50 large industrial companies, having 1959 contributions totaling $63 million, it was found that 41 per cent went to education. In 1955 the International Harvester Foundation gave 11 per cent of its grants to education; by 1958 the figure had jumped to 22 per cent.

Suggestions and Recommendations

The company-sponsored foundation has some unique features which affect its manner of operation, but its place in society is essentially the same as that of all other kinds of *private* foundations. Like other foundations—to borrow Leonard Mayo's terminology—it has five basic functions: exploration, initiation and demonstration, communication, mobilization of support, and evaluation. The writer offers a few observations under these headings.

Company-sponsored foundations ought to *explore* promising leads in research and experimentation. They should *initiate and demonstrate* new or untested programs. They should of course *communicate* their activities and their plans, for the guidance of prospective grant applicants and to help government groups and other foundations with program planning.

Company-sponsored foundations can often perform a vital function by *mobilizing support:* private foundations, other agencies, and even government often need to pool their resources and talents to reach an important objective. The matter of public versus private concerns is a gray area, no longer a black and white one. As Novice Fawcett, President of Ohio State University, has said, institutions such as his are better described as "tax-assisted" rather than "tax-supported"; Ohio State now derives less than half its non-business income from tax sources. The Midwest Airborne Television experiment, initiated by The Ford Foundation, is another example of a project so large and complex as to require joint effort by many groups including foundations, private and public educational institutions, as well as federal, state, and local governments.

Company-sponsored foundations should *evaluate* and review their own programs, as well as the current status of the fields in which they operate. Most such foundations are understaffed. They would help themselves, and the causes they support, by reducing their grants 2 or 3 per cent and spending that money on additional staff—people to help do the investigative and creative work so that the remaining 97 or 98 per cent may be given more wisely.

Finally, if the private sector in our society is to be kept strong and effective, company-sponsored foundations ought to do several essential things. First and foremost, in this crisis decade, they should work for the strengthening of our educational system. Some large companies which are still hold-outs and thousands of medium-sized and smaller companies which extend no such support must be induced to get into the act. In addition to this primary direction, company-sponsored foundations must strive to make their giving more purposeful, giving according to deliberately conceived plans rather than in response to personal pressures and daily demands. Flexibility should be carefully preserved: there is a regrettable tendency among companies and their foundations to make some contributions only because they have been making them for years.

The need for *creativity* in spending foundation resources deserves special emphasis. One of the most recent examples to come to my attention is a small project of The Johnson Foundation, not strictly a company-sponsored foundation but set up by S. C. Johnson & Son, Inc. In addition to designing the famous office building for the makers of Johnson's wax, Frank Lloyd Wright also created the Johnson family home. This has recently been presented to the Foundation, which intends to use it as a sort of midwest "Arden House" where groups of 15 to 20 people can convene in "think" sessions on current problems. Another example is that of the CBS Foundation, providing one-year News and Public Affairs Fellowships which include not only study at Columbia University but also make use of the extensive facilities of CBS radio and television, giving Fellows on-the-job training of a high order.

Our knowledge of company-sponsored foundations is relatively scanty. But there is evidence that they are already filling a vital role in philanthropy with a total impact for good far greater than the dollars they contribute.

Preparing the Foundation Proposal

MANNING M. PATTILLO*

LET US MAKE two assumptions. First, I take it that we are talking primarily about the large, professionally staffed foundations that are trying to do a systematic job of philanthropy and have expertness in the field of higher education. The company foundation and the small family foundation are usually quite different from the general welfare foundation in their purposes and mode of operation.

Secondly, let us assume that the institution seeking funds has analyzed its needs in terms of foundation policy. This seems obvious enough, but many colleges and universities fail to do it. There are some types of assistance that fit into the pattern of giving of large foundations, and others that ordinarily do not. It is usually unrealistic to expect to secure grants for general support, or buildings, or endowment, from the larger foundations. There are some exceptions. For example, The Kresge Foundation and the Olin Foundation have given substantially toward college and university building funds. Also, the broad provisions of the Special Program of The Ford Foundation may be mentioned. But, as a general rule, the larger foundations contribute little or nothing for current operations, buildings, and endowment. Foundations of the type we are discussing usually make grants only for programs or projects that cannot be financed from the grantee's regular budget or from individual donors. Examining the financial statements of large foundations, one may get an impression of unlimited funds, but the fact is that these foundations have resources which are small in relation to the demands made upon them; as a matter of policy they usually give preference to undertakings of an experimental or research character, holding promise of significant advances in education or scholarship. They do not have the money to give broad support for the on-going work of colleges and universities.

It is not my business to justify this policy. I know as well as anyone else that such a policy *can* lead to frothy, cooked-up, visionary schemes that will

* The Danforth Foundation; previously Associate Director, Lilly Endowment. Mr. Pattillo's remarks are excerpted from an address before the Foundation Relations Workshop of the American College Public Relations Association, New York City, 12–13 November 1962; a full text is included in *Understanding Foundation Support for Higher Education*, ed. Leo C. Muller (ACPRA, 1963).

result in little or no solid accomplishment, but this is not inherent in the policy, and it is the intention of soundly administered foundations to separate the carefully conceived, workable proposals from the superficial, the poorly planned, the inconsequential. I think it is best for the applicant to operate on the assumption that he is dealing with people of good judgment who know what they are doing.

This means that the individual undergraduate college (as distinguished from the university) is at a disadvantage in securing foundation grants. One can lament this—and I do—but it is simply a fact of life in raising funds from foundations, and nothing is gained by pretending that it is not so. Universities with extensive graduate programs have a distinct advantage in attracting foundation grants because they are engaged in activities that lend themselves to foundation support.

Essential Ingredients

Now, there is nothing mystical about foundation proposals. There are no trade secrets or magical formulas. (If I were choosing a sub-title for my remarks, it would be "A Plea for Common Sense.") The main thing is to have an idea and a clearly thought out plan of action to accomplish something important in education or scholarship. The project or program should be concisely described in straightforward English, with a minimum of technical jargon. Remember that the proposal will probably be read not only by specialists but also by intelligent laymen. It should include a statement of purposes and why they are important; how they are to be achieved; what specific results may be expected; what persons will direct the work; how much it will cost; and, usually, why this particular institution or agency is the proper one to undertake the project or program. The proposal itself or a covering letter should provide assurance that the plans have the backing of the president or other appropriate officer of the organization that would administer the funds. In the great majority of cases the essential facts can be stated in three or four pages. If it takes much more space than that to outline the proposal, probably it has not been thought through sufficiently. Without wishing to state this as an axiom, I can say that in almost every instance I have seen of a voluminous proposal requiring a large amount of paper, the lack of brevity seemed to indicate that the drafters of the proposal could not see clearly the essentials of their plans. They were bogged down in details or were muddy in their thinking, or a great deal of verbiage was being used to make up for a deficiency of real substance.

Too Many Words

There are some fields (I dare not name them; you probably know them as well as I) which are particularly given to wordiness and offensive jargon;

the practitioners find it difficult to state even the least complicated notions briefly in simple English. In my experience these are also the fields in which one can expect the lowest return on the philanthropic dollar. The outcomes of projects and programs in these fields are all too often as nebulous and hazy and inconclusive as the proposals. The experience of foundations in this connection is not unique. You probably see the same thing in budget requests coming to the administration within your institution. And you know your own reaction to a request that will not "come clear," that you cannot visualize clearly in your mind after carefully studying the plans.

During the six years in which I was involved in the grant-making process, I had occasion to summarize hundreds of proposals from colleges and universities, involving a variety of scholarly fields. I found that, for internal purposes, I could usually summarize the essential facts in one or two typewritten pages. Often the best proposals could be reduced to one paragraph.

I am not saying that foundations judge applications by their brevity. What I am suggesting is that, when you are preparing a proposal, if reams and reams of paper are required to outline the request, probably the plans have not come to a sharp enough focus to enable you to make a convincing case for support to a critical outsider who is accustomed to evaluating educational proposals.

Some grant-making organizations have a printed form or prescribe a certain order of items in application for funds. Others leave it to the applicant to write the proposal as he sees fit. These are details of procedure. The main thing is to state concisely and clearly what it is you want to do and how it is to be done. There is no need, in dealing with the better foundations, to "doll up" the proposal in leather binding with silver braid and gold lettering. This is just window dressing and is not likely to impress an experienced foundation officer. He will be much more interested in the substance than in the trimmings. Too much attention to appearances may seem to reflect bad taste or a preoccupation with trivialities.

Some Helpful Preliminaries

All of us are acutely aware of the fact that a tremendous amount of time is spent by faculty members and administrators developing proposals for submission to foundations. Since many of these proposals never lead to grants, much staff time is wasted in unproductive activity. I believe that, if the suggestions I made earlier about screening financial needs in terms of foundation policies were followed, some of this waste could be obviated. There is a tendency, particularly in the larger universities, to turn to foundations uncritically whenever any faculty member would like to launch something new. Every university has a few men who are almost professional "grant-seekers," spending a good fraction of their time "dreaming up" projects to attract foundation money. Undoubtedly, a reduction in this activity would be advantageous all along the line. It would save valuable faculty time, cut down on the torrent of paper flowing into foundation offices, and eliminate unnecessary projects that might, somehow, actually find support.

There are other ways in which time can be saved. The scholar or administrator, especially one who has had previous relations with a given foundation and who knows and is known by the foundation officers, can often save everyone's time by an informal approach, outlining quite briefly in a letter what he has in mind and asking frankly whether the possibility of foundation interest is such as to justify a more formal request. Sometimes even a telephone call will accomplish the purpose.

Also, it seems to me that paper-work could be greatly reduced if applicants submitted proposals to foundations one at a time rather than simultaneously. Often a request is sent to eight or ten foundations at the same time, with the hope that one of them may show interest. This kind of mass solicitation is expensive in foundation staff time and occasionally leads to embarrassment. I recall a proposal that was submitted by a respected university to two foundations simultaneously and resulted in two grants. The administration was in the awkward position of having to apologize and decline one of the grants. The circumstances were almost such as to raise ethical questions. Certainly, the university should have kept both foundations informed of the progress of its efforts.

I would predict that the future will see some attempt at the development of an effective code of ethics for educational fund-raising. Many institutions are engaging in practices that are unworthy of higher education. I am entirely sympathetic with hard-pressed administrators who have the almost impossible task of finding sufficient money to finance their institutions. They are often unsung heroes. But I still believe that the manipulative attitude toward donors, which is all too prevalent, is doing something to the dignity of college and university administration. I suspect that there is many an administrator who would be a little ashamed to confide even to his wife some of the tricky practices he has used to get money. Probably foundations are less subject and susceptible to dubious methods of fund-raising than are individual donors. It seems to me that, even though it may cost us urgently needed money, we owe it to the honorable tradition of higher education to be gentlemen. Lest it seem that I am too harsh on people seeking money, let me say that I could cite a few foundations—fortunately not among the better known ones—that might well do some soul-searching with respect to their treatment of applicants.

Follow-Ups

What can we say about follow-up of proposals? Once a request is submitted to a foundation, the initiative usually lies with the prospective donor. Someone on the foundation staff will acknowledge the application and either say that a grant cannot be made or suggest that the matter be pursued in conversation or by submission of additional information. The institution may be invited to send a representative to the foundation offices, or a foundation staff person may visit the institution. A reasonably prompt reply can normally be expected from the better organized foundations.

Every foundation has its own procedure for initial consideration of applications. The decision as to what further steps, if any, should be taken will usually rest with a staff committee or an officer of the foundation. Often, if specialized expertness is required for a proper evaluation, the proposal will be referred to outside scholars in whose judgment the foundation has confidence. The proposal will be examined in the light of board policy, funds currently available for new grants, the merit of the proposal itself, other proposals and plans before the foundation, commitments already made for projects and programs, and perhaps other factors.

It is important to note—and I emphasize this—that the intrinsic value of the proposal is only one of several factors that will govern the foundation's action. Applicants often do not understand this. They feel that they have a splendid project or program and that that is sufficient to assure favorable action. If the request is declined, they are likely to conclude that the foundation did not appreciate the importance of the proposal. Most of the larger foundations face the unhappy necessity of declining many sound requests simply because the funds are not currently available to support all the good proposals. The purpose of clear policies defining a foundation's areas of interest is to make the choices as fair and rational as possible.

It is also important to recognize that the foundation officer or officers who act on applications are doing their best to interpret the wishes of their board of trustees. Foundation staff members are not free to do as they please about individual requests any more than administrative officers of colleges and universities are in a position to operate on the basis of personal impulse. Both carry on their work within a framework of institutional policy which is ultimately determined by a board. In most of the foundations with which I am acquainted, affirmative actions on requests, or at least the larger requests, require board action. It is well to bear in mind that the unwillingness of a foundation representative to give you a definite answer—yes or no—on a request in the early stages of consideration, is probably due to the fact that he is not himself sure what the final decision will be. Even if the foundation staff is much impressed with a given proposal and recommends it heartily to the board, authorization of the grant is not thereby guaranteed. The process of decision-making in large foundations is more intricate than most applicants realize. A number of factors properly influence the action on a particular request.

Foundation Diversity

If a request is turned down by a foundation, the proper thing is to thank them for their consideration of the matter and then look for another appropriate foundation. This advice cannot be stressed too strongly. There are some 15,000 foundations in the United States. An applicant with a promising proposal, and persistence, can almost always secure the funds required, sooner or later. He should not get discouraged after one or two rejections unless basic weaknesses in the proposal have been uncovered in the process of negotiation. If two or three experienced foundation officers, in frank conversation, say that they think the proposal is a strong one but that their foundations, for reasons which do not reflect unfavorably on the proposal, must decline the request, this encouragement should stimulate the applicant to pursue his search for a grant. The inexperienced applicant is likely to become discouraged and give up too soon. Persistence should be shown, however, not in attempting to brow-beat the foundation that has already taken a negative action but in approaching other foundations. This is "follow-through" in its proper sense.

Most colleges and universities have too narrow a view of foundations. The common assumption is that there are only ten or a dozen foundations that count. Actually, the field is much broader than that. There are many requests that might more appropriately be submitted to a small or medium-sized foundation than to the big foundations, which are inundated with appeals. Where a college or university has a special officer on foundation relations, I should think that one of the most useful things that he could do would be to explore relations with a broader group of foundations, including smaller foundations in the immediate region. It should be remembered that, while the larger foundations have more substantial resources, they also have greater demands made upon them. A smaller foundation that is less well known may be an excellent prospect in connection with a particular request.

How Foundations Evaluate Requests

YORKE ALLEN, JR.*

FOR THOSE who have asked foundations for grants, it may be of interest to gain some idea of the questions which arise in the mind of a foundation executive as he gazes at the pile of requests stacked on his desk in front of him. Here, as briefly as possible, are seven steps which may be taken in a foundation before an affirmative decision is reached concerning a proposal.

Step 1—Judging Significance

The first step in the evaluation process is to analyze the proposal and ascertain its essential significance. Foundation executives are obliged to review many and varied appeals in the course of a day. Hence, fund raisers are right in suggesting that the initial written request or covering letter should be short—one or two pages—describing the proposition accurately and completely. It is also helpful when the organization making an appeal attaches to its request a balance sheet, income statement, and budgetary estimates setting forth its own financial position.

If a college president sends a letter asking, let us say, for a grant of $500,000 with which to build a dormitory, there is not much difficulty analyzing such an appeal. But the evaluation of proposals involving specialized research or brand new projects in the field of human values is not so easy. If these projects have never previously been attempted, all of the important aspects and consequences of their operations must be accurately conceptualized. Occasionally, it is not even a simple matter to evaluate the work of a well established and highly regarded agency. In the case of one agency in the field of social relations, I talked with three of its officials over a period of six months but was unable to obtain from them what was for me a sufficiently clear impression of the factors which made that organization "tick." Recently the agency's director stopped by our office for the first time, and as a result of his account of his day-to-day activities it finally became clear to me why this organization is so successful in its work.

* Associate, Rockefeller Brothers Fund. This material is adapted from an address at the "Conference on Voluntary Giving for American Christian Institutions," 13 February 1964.

The foundation executive must distinguish on the one hand between projects which are plausible and articulately described but lack substance, and those proposals on the other hand which seem to have some real or potential merit but also suffer important defects. In this sorting out process, it is curious how an agency's financial statements will disclose not only its fiscal position but also its administrative efficiency: a complex financial statement frequently reflects an obsolete organizational structure, or overlapping and ineffective operating procedures; whereas a simple, straightforward format often indicates efficient management.

As a means of judging the degree to which a requesting organization is committed to its proposal, a foundation executive will check to see if the request has been sent by the head of that organization or by one of its subordinate officials. In the latter case, the subordinate may be the only person interested in the appeal. But even when the request is signed by the president, executive director, or general secretary, the signature may merely indicate their concurrence with the request rather than wholehearted support for it.

Step 2—Does It Fit?

Then the foundation executive must decide whether the project will fit into his foundation's program or budget. Many worthwhile proposals must be declined either because (1) the foundation is not concerned with those particular fields of endeavor, or (2) it has no funds available at the moment to underwrite the cost of a particular project, or (3) it cannot contribute additional funds to the requesting agency, or for that type of activity, without upsetting the program balance between the foundation's various fields of interest.

Step 3—Any Duplication?

The third step is to ascertain whether the project proposes to duplicate an operation or service already being performed by an existing agency. Many foundation executives are generalists; they know a bit about what is going on in a wide variety of fields. At the same time they ought to be specialists in at least one field so that they can point to or define with some precision its so called "growing edges." Foundation executives also find it useful to have a network of consultants on whom they may call formally or informally for advice on a confidential basis. In addition, they can and often do save a great deal of time by comparing notes with their opposite numbers in other foundations active in the same field. Despite the difficulty which most outsiders have in following and trying to understand the pattern of activities of a given foundation, it rarely (if ever) happens that a grant made by one fund unnecessarily overlaps or duplicates a grant made by another fund.

Step 4—Possible Results

Now comes the task of considering what would be likely to result if the proposed project actually came to be implemented. A foundation executive may take a negative or positive approach when analyzing this phase of the problem. He may ask himself, "If this new venture is not undertaken, what harm would be done?" Or he may ask the officials of a requesting agency, "Suppose you received the necessary money and completed your project; what useful results do you believe would emerge from it?" Sometimes they reply: "If you give us the money, we'll find out the answer." This is what I call a "blank check" type of request, and few foundations find them attractive. On the other hand, in the case of appeals for support for "pure" as opposed to "applied" research projects, a foundation is obliged to ignore this factor and rely instead on the professional reputation of the individuals proposing the projects.

A foundation executive usually wants to have a timetable for a new proposal submitted to him so that he may have some idea when the venture will hopefully be completed. Sometimes it is necessary for him to guess whether it may subsequently be necessary for him to keep in close touch with a researcher or organization officials. This is particularly so if he thinks the latter may have difficulty bringing the new venture to a successful conclusion.

Another question which is asked during the appraisal of a project is whether it has any "multiplier" value inherent in it. In other words, if the proposal proves to be a success, what is the likelihood that more than one institution or organization will benefit from it?

Step 5—Question of Cost

At this point the dollar sign enters the equation. Would the proposed undertaking be worth its estimated cost? In the case of a proposed new building the answer to this question is not hard to find. But for projects related to the promotion of human values, the attempt to equate estimated costs with hoped-for results can be a troublesome process. In fact, beyond a point, it is impossible.

For example, I recall having fussed for almost two years over a request from an organization which was then known as the National Council for Religion in Higher Education. The Council operated a rather unusual fellowship program (called the Kent Fellowship) in the field of religion in higher education. It took two of my associates and myself over two years to agree that the price tag involved in this proposal was reasonable in terms of the results being achieved by the program. Eventually we became convinced on this point and a grant was made to that organization.

A foundation executive also considers whether the backers of a proposed new project might be able to obtain the needed sums of money from their own resources. In other words, what priority does the requesting agency place on its own proposal? If it assigns a low priority, the proposal is probably not worth implementing. On the other hand, if a large organization making an appeal assigns a top priority to a new venture, the chances are it should try to pay for it out of its own resources, and, if necessary, eliminate some low-priority item from its overall budget in order to be able to do so. Thus, in this sense, contributions from foundations might often be considered marginal money.

Most foundation executives like to analyze the budget of a project in some detail. The heading and price-tag assigned to each item in the budget provide a good means of judging which of the project's component elements may be safely eliminated without jeopardizing prospects for its success.

In this connection, I recall an appeal we received not long ago for a new venture in an important area of scholarship. The project impressed us as being worthwhile in most respects except that several items within its budget appeared to be more costly than necessary. When I asked the professor heading the project about it, he smiled and replied he had been advised that one should always "pad" a request to a foundation. After I pointed out the places I thought were padded, he agreed to revise the budget downward. Ultimately we contributed one-half the amount requested. And I am glad to say this venture is now proceeding successfully.

Step 6—Management Evaluation

Assuming that the project survives all the tests outlined above, the next question is will its proponents be able to carry out the proposal effectively? Most organizations reflect the personalities and operate in accordance with the capabilities of their leaders. Therefore, after screening the initial written request, it is crucial for the foundation executive to have several personal interviews with the key persons making the proposal. I can recall in a number of instances listening to requests being endorsed orally by what might be called "big names" in business and other fields, when in the space of a few minutes of conversation it became almost painfully evident that the top brass actually knew comparatively little about the operations of the agency and were only lending a brief amount of their time to it. On the other hand, if a person of eminent stature presents a request with which he demonstrates true familiarity, this can be an important factor in evaluating a proposal favorably.

The foundation executive may also visit the office of the organization making the appeal, or an institution's campus. It is curious how differently some people appear in their own offices than they do while waiting for the foundation receptionist to usher them into the "inner sanctum!" So much of the business of administering philanthropy consists in sizing up persons and estimating the potential worth of their output in the future that I believe this sixth step in the appraisal process is the most important one of all.

Step 7—Selling the Project

The last step taken by a foundation executive in evaluating a request occurs after he is personally "sold" on the idea of making a grant but begins to wonder whether he in turn can "sell" the project to other members of his staff or to his own trustees. In the case of the large foundation this process may involve the use of "program committees" in appraising an appeal. The membership of such a committee may include one or more of the fund's officers as well as several staff personnel specializing in various fields. The idea is that an "interdisciplinary" type of review (similar to oral examinations given to candidates for doctoral degrees) is likely to result in a more comprehensive consideration and screening of the appeal.

The problem confronting foundation trustees who wish to evaluate requests in depth is not an easy one. In the case of the larger foundations, trustee meeting agenda usually contain dockets outlining such a variety of proposals that the trustees cannot be expected to explore all of them in any great detail. Consequently, much depends on the degree of confidence they place in the members of the staff. In the typical foundation I believe the trustees are usually inclined to go along with most recommendations on the grounds that the details of many projects are technical in nature, and that the chief functions of a trustee are to define overall policies and to make sure that the staff abides by them. But this is not a universal rule, and occasionally a trustee is likely to take a very lively interest in evaluating a proposal which happens to fall within the area of his own particular vocation or special competence.

In conclusion, I would summarize by saying that once the proposals sent to foundations have been screened out and the unsuitable ones declined, the process of evaluating the comparatively few remaining requests consists in assisting in the structuring of new projects by attempting to envision and provide for all of the operational features needed to help make these ventures a success. In this process the conveyance of the funds granted by a foundation is the last but by no means the most important step; and when discussing an appeal, particularly in instances where it is not possible to make a grant, foundation executives try to be as helpful as they can.

INDEX

Index